Adolescent Runaways

Adolescent Runaways

Causes and Consequences

Mark-David Janus
University of Connecticut

Arlene McCormack
University of Lowell

Ann Wolbert Burgess
University of Pennsylvania

Carol Hartman
Boston College

Lexington Books
D.C. Heath and Company/Lexington, Massachusetts/Toronto

We appreciate the support for data analysis provided from Grant No. 84–JN–AX–K010 from the Office of Juvenile Justice and Delinquency Prevention, Office of Justice Assistance, Research, and Statistics, U.S. Department of Justice. Points of view or opinions in this book are ours and do not necessarily represent the official position or policies of the U.S. Department of Justice.

Library of Congress Cataloging-in-Publication Data

Adolescent runaways.

Bibliography: p.
Includes index.
1. Runaway youth. 2. Runaway youth—Canada.
3. Runaway youth—Services for—Planning. I. Janus, Mark-David.
HV715.A37   1987   362.7'4   86–45037
ISBN 0–669–13047–8 (alk. paper)
ISBN 0–669–15280–3 (pbk. : alk. paper)

Published simultaneously in Canada
Printed in the United States of America
Casebound International Standard Book Number: 0–669–13047–8
Paperbound International Standard Book Number: 0–669–15280–3
Library of Congress Catalog Card Number: 86–45037

The paper used in this publication meets the minimum requirements of American National Standard for Information Sciences—Permanence of Paper for Printed Library Materials, ANSI Z39.48–1984. ∞™

87 88 89 90 8 7 6 5 4 3 2 1

*To Dan, Pammy, Dave, and Marie and to all their American
and Canadian sisters and brothers who, like themselves, are
running for their lives*

Contents

Foreword

Covenant House, New York, and Under-21, Toronto, are pleased to have cosponsored this research on runaway and homeless youth with the U.S. Office of Juvenile Justice and Delinquency Prevention. It is crucial that professional attention be directed toward this ever-growing number of vulnerable and abused children.

We hope that contributions to the professional literature will stimulate increased interest in homeless and runaway youth, provoking new models of response and prevention. The lives of these youth tell their own story and the story of our society. It is encumbent on us all to listen to the story runaway youth are paying with their lives to tell.

—*Father Bruce Ritter,* President
Covenant House

Acknowledgments

We wish to acknowledge the many people and agencies who have helped us with this project. We would like to thank first the Rev. Bruce Ritter of Covenant House, New York; his assistant, S. Gretchen Gilroy; and the staff of Covenant House-Toronto, particularly Mary McConville, Michael Faye, and Chad Hanna, whose vision, support, and participation made this research possible.

We are grateful for the data assistance provided by research assistants Hollyjean Chaplick, Christine Grant, Sidney Henkel, Daniel Hannon, and Karen Woelfel, and for the computer assistance of Peter Gaccione. We are especially indebted to the careful and precise editorial attention provided by Marieanne L. Clark.

We very much appreciated the support and encouragement of our respective universities: the University of Connecticut Library research staff, and the administrators at the University of Lowell, the University of Pennsylvania, and Boston College. Additionally, we would like to thank the Paulist Fathers, particularly those in Boston, Toronto, and Storrs, and the community of St. Thomas Aquinas for their personal encouragement.

— Mark-David Janus

1
Runaway Youth in the Twentieth Century

Running away from home is often considered a normal part of childhood, as depicted in *The Adventures of Tom Sawyer*. Many people recall episodes when they packed a lunch, took the family dog, and ran away from home, only to return at suppertime or as dark drew near. Angry with inappreciative parents, children throughout the years have been jealous of Tom Sawyer's opportunity to come home after running away and be the guest of honor at his own funeral:

> As the service proceeded, the clergyman drew such pictures of the graces, the winning ways, and the rare promises of the lost lads that every soul there, thinking he recognized these pictures, felt a pang in remembering that he had persistently blinded himself to them always before and had as persistently seen only faults and flaws in the poor boys. The Minister related many a touching incident in the lives of the departed, too, which illustrated their sweet generous natures, and the people could easily see, now, how noble and beautiful these episodes were, and remembered with grief that at the time they occurred they seemed rank rascalities, well deserving of cowhide. The congregation became more and more moved, as the pathetic tale went on, till, at last, the whole company broke down and joined the weeping mourners in a chorus of anguished sobs, the preacher himself giving way to his feelings and crying in the pulpit.[1]

Tom Sawyer, Huckleberry Finn, Oliver Twist, David Copperfield, Horatio Alger—these are the waifs and orphans who, in the popular imagination, define the runaway youth. This mischievous child, the adventurer, the orphan, the survivor, and the hero all play a part in our perceptions of the youth who runs away from home. These figures have served to characterize the runaway as an endearing—if immature—child who has lost his way and who needs to be gathered back into the nest.

Yet running away from home in contemporary society has little to do with experiences such as those of Tom Sawyer. Professional interactions with runaways have resulted in other descriptions of these youths: psychoneurotic,

sociopathic, psychopathic, antagonistic, undisciplined, impulsive, delinquent, and depressed.

Whether running away from home should be viewed as a delinquent, if
more or less normal, part of adolescent development or whether it is indicative of a pathological condition became a question of increasing importance
in the United States during the 1960s and 1970s, a time when the numbers of
youths who were leaving their homes seemed to rise dramatically. The shape
and tone of this rising concern is evident in articles appearing at the time
in general publications and in published hearings and reports of the U.S.
Congress.

Changing Perspectives

A May 10, 1964, article in the *New York Times Magazine* is typical of the
attitude toward runaways during the early and mid 1960s. The article noted
that the number of runaways was increasing and that these runaways,
included "a surprising number of good students," inferring that the popular
belief was that only troubled youths were expected to engage in such delinquent behavior.[2] The article also stated that running away, far from signaling
that anything is wrong in the home, "is a smoke screen for the child's wish to
come back on his terms" and that the child running from home is, in fact,
"running to a fancied adventure."[3]

The runaway child was discussed again in 1967, not with emphasis on
the situation the child leaves, but rather with attention to where runaways go
after they leave home and with the increase in runaways associated with a
general youth rebellion. *Life* magazine, in its November 3, 1967, issue,
presented an extensive photo essay on runaway youths living in the East
Greenwich Village of New York City, hinting that the life of a runaway child
was not as carefree or romantic as frequently suggested.[4] In an October 30,
1967, issue, *Newsweek* also discussed runaways as youths in search of
"hippieland" who may instead find themselves exposed to drugs, gangs, and
violence.[5] After noting that Chicago police reported that they were handling
50 percent more runaways than five years earlier, *Time* magazine also
described runaways spending their time in hippie crash pads. According to
Time, the carefree image of the runaway was becoming associated with an
image of conflict and pain, which somehow could prevent the youth from
returning home: "Time was when parents almost took it for granted that any
red-blooded boy would sooner or later run away from home on a summer
time Tom Sawyer adventure. . . . But for an increasing number of tormented
teenagers, running away is not a lark, but a serious act for which returning
home is an all but unthinkable conclusion."[6]

In 1972, *US News & World Report* began a series of six major reports on runaway youth, a series that would extend until 1979. The first of these articles revealed a definite shift in analysis and alarm. It was reported that although the campus violence and youth unrest associated with runaways were slackening, the incidence of runaways was increasing. (The number of suburban runaways was up 90% in Evanston, Illinois.) The article presented two different reactions to this phenomenon. On one hand, running away was still seen as a capricious, immature act, a "form of blackmail that the kid uses on the parent. Maybe the parent won't let the kid stay out as late as he wants, so he runs away. Some of these parents have taken threats from their kids since they were small. They ought to call the kid's bluff and not give in."[7] On the other hand, the article sounded a note of alarm: "Compared to six months ago many more of the kids we're seeing are from working classes. This means the fadism of running away is over. Kids who are running away now have more serious difficulties to run from. It's harder to get them back into their families than before."[8]

The concern about runaways reached significant enough proportions to merit a hearing before the 1972 Senate Subcommittee on Juvenile Justice. The committee's opening statement, made by Senator Birch Bayh, summarized the growing national concern:

> When Mark Twain pictured Huckleberry Finn and Tom Sawyer floating down the Mississippi River he was responding to a well established American tradition. Running away has always been part of America's folklore. For many of our young people, it has served as a part of their rite of passage into adulthood.
>
> Today, however, running away is less likely to be a healthy striving for adulthood than an anguished cry for help from a child who has nowhere else to turn. Experts agree that most runaways are not involved in a healthy search for mature identity. Instead they are escaping from serious problems at home, at school, or within themselves.
>
> The act of running away calls attention to the problems, but it rarely leads to a solution. The runaway who is returned home against his will is more likely to represent a problem postponed than a problem solved. However, forcible return is the only solution made available by most institutions that now deal with runaways.
>
> If running away is likely to be an unhealthy escape from problems, it is a far less safe solution than it was in the past. A runaway today literally has no friends. If he is under 18, he is probably violating the law. Thus, most runaways are subject to arrest by the police and may well be incarcerated in a juvenile institution, or even an adult jail. . . .
>
> Because the runaway problem is largely ignored in our society, a young person seriously endangers himself when he leaves home. Unlike Mark Twain's era, running away today is a phenomenon of our cities. Most runaways are young, inexperienced suburban kids who runaway to major urban areas. New York, San Francisco, Washington, Boston, Atlanta and many

other cities receive the bulk of the runaway population. The children who run to these cities look for companionship, friendship and approval from the people they meet. Instead they often become the easy victims of street gangs, drug pushers, and hardened criminals. Without adequate shelter and food, they are prey to a whole range of medical ills from upper respiratory infections to venereal disease. One wonders what a modern version of *The Adventures of Huckleberry Finn* would be like, or even if it would be permitted reading in our schools.[9]

The committee heard testimony describing what became identified as the prototypal runaway environment of East Greenwich Village, emphasizing the unforseen dangers there:

Greenwich Village in the last twenty years has moved from the Bohemian element, through the Beatnick to the Hippie or Flower Culture. To many folks it is a subculture, or radical departure from the status quo of society or the "Establishment" per se. . . . Youth flock to this area by the thousands in order to be part of the action. They come in droves from rural, urban and suburban areas alike. Figures range from five to seven hundred in winter to well over two thousand in the warm months. They view the sleazy streets, the night life, the rock music and the discotheques as a haven for excitement and fulfillment. So enchanting and luring is the attraction than their responsibilities to family and home, the pursuit of education and responsibility in general becomes secondary to satiation of lustful quests. . . . A preposterous fantasy about the life in communal centers has grown up. TV and teen movies show relaxed, happy kids playing cops and robbers with stupid police, foolish parents, and invariably winning. No hint is ever given of the unbelievable filth, greed, violence, and endless hours of boredom awaiting most runaways. They pour into the East Village and its counterparts in other parts of the country in search of the freedom they think they were deprived of at home, and find an iron fisted boss in every crash pad, and rigid code to which they must conform if they are to survive. In the movies the crash boss is depicted as a sweetly reasonable father figure whose one concern is to help everyone to do exactly as he pleases. It doesn't take them long to find out how things really are. Particularly the girls among them find that in the name of free love their most casual boy-girl attraction is expected to be consummated in sexual experience, very often deviate and degrading. . . . From this to actual prostitution is a very short step. Both boys and girls learn quickly that experimentation with drugs, if not actual addiction, is necessary in order to become accepted as part of a "family," the name by which groups who live together in a common crash pad are called.[10]

In the face of such alarming testimony of the dangers awaiting runaway youths when they leave home, the Senate Subcommittee on Juvenile Justice sponsored S2829, the Runaway Youth Act, which found that:

(1) the number of juveniles who leave and remain away from home without parental permission has increased to alarming proportions, creating a significant law enforcement problem for the communities inundated, and significantly endangering the young people who are without resources and live on the street;

(2) that the exact nature of the problem is not well defined because national statistics on the size and profile of the runaway population are not tabulated;

(3) that many of these young people, because of their age and situation are urgently in need of temporary shelter and counseling services;

(4) that the anxieties and fears of parents whose children have run away from home can best be alleviated by the effective interstate services and the earliest possible contact with their children;

(5) that the problem of locating, detaining, and returning runaway children should not be the responsibility of already overburdened police departments and juvenile justice authorities; and

(6) that in the view of the interstate nature of the problem, it is the responsibility of the Federal Government to develop accurate reporting of the problem nationally and to develop an effective system of temporary care outside the law enforcement structure.[11]

Clearly, runaways were now seen as at risk on the street and as belonging at home as soon as they could be returned there. Despite this concern, no action on S2829 was effected until the horrifying 1973 murders of runaway and homeless youths by Dean Coryell and Wayne Henley. Both *Time* (August 27, 1973) and *US News & World Report* (September 3, 1973) printed extensive articles expressing outrage that Houston police did so little to find the missing boys and prevent the tragedy.[12,13]

Strong public opinion promoted legislation, and in 1974 Congress and the president responded to rising concern over the numbers of youths who were leaving home without parental permission, who were crossing state lines, and who were exposed to exploitation and other dangers while on the run. The Runaway Youth Act authorized the secretary of health, education, and welfare to award grants for the development or support of new or existing centers designed to address the immediate needs of runaways.

During the first year of the Runaway Youth Act, 120 programs were begun. Approximately 33,000 youths were sheltered, and 22,000 runaways used a national runaway hotline to contact their parents. From these youths came a wealth of information about runaways. Oversight hearings that evaluated the first year of service included testimony on youths with what was then considered "special needs": histories of abuse by parents and guardians and needs for shelter, food, medical care, and legal advice. It was reported that 56 percent of the runaways served by the centers had traveled less than fifty miles from their homes. Running away appeared to be at least as much a home-town issue as a national issue. In addition, for the first time those youths who might not be able to return home were discussed. The funded shelters were designed to provide temporary care and counseling, but shelter workers discovered that some runaways needed independent living situations as well as long-term counseling and support after they had returned home.[14]

The oversight report noted that clinical experience after just one year of service identified the family as a participant in the crisis previously attributed to failures in the individual youths:

> Gone is the phenomenon of the 1960's seeking new life styles and communes for mutual needs, in its place is exploitation, abuse and a multi-billion dollar sex industry. . . . Youth leaving home are experiencing a multitude of family related problems and . . . "running away" constitutes only one act of a number of acts which have placed the youth and family in crisis. . . . An increasing number of runaway youth have family related problems which stem from being without a supportive stable home environment. Many runaway youth projects report large increases in the number of homeless youth.[15]

The print media immediately noted the differences between popular myth and the reality of runaways. The number of runaway youths continued to increase, with *US News & World Report* stating on May 12, 1975, that "America's tide of runaway children—many of them "push outs," encouraged by their parents to leave home, rolls on unchecked. . . . Running away, for more and more children, is becoming an escape from home conditions they find intolerable, not a quest for adventure, pleasure or socio-political protest as happened during the hippie era of the 1960's.[16]

Runaways at Risk

Continued clinical experience not only clarified the difficult situations that face runaways at home, but also revealed in graphic fashion the dangers of child prostitution and pornography that face runaways on the street. *Time* magazine's article "Children's Garden of Perversity" (April 4, 1977) and CBS Television's "Sixty Minutes" segment "Kiddie Porn" brought into American homes stories of the manufacture of child pornography and of prostitution, as told by youths involved.[17,18] In addition, the *Chicago Tribune* reported on an investigation into child pornography and prostitution, a report that ran in a four-part series from May 15–18 that same year.[19]

These accounts led to a hearing on the protection of children against sexual exploitation before the Subcommittee to Investigate Juvenile Delinquency of the Senate Committee of the Judiciary on May 27 and June 16, 1977. The opening statement of Iowa senator John Culver described the new state of knowledge that had evolved in the three years since the 1974 runaway act was passed:

> During the past several years, a new menace has mushroomed into big business in America . . . the exploitation of young boys and girls for the purpose of producing pornography. . . . It is estimated that there are some 700,000–1,000,000 runaway juveniles in the country at the present moment. . . . Millions of cases of child abuse each year have led to the alienation of young people from their parents. And against this backdrop is the breakdown of the family and the fundamental values of our society. Questions must be asked of the adequacy of our educational system, the effectiveness of our social agencies, the responsibility or lack of responsibility being demonstrated by American parents in their marriage relationships, our ability to deal with poverty and unemployment in America and the quality of our justice system.[20]

The hearings themselves focused extensively on the connections between teenage prostitution, pornography, and runaways. The committee interviewed a male street prostitute, local police, and convicted pornographers.

The committee heard testimony that male runaway youths might become involved in prostitution in as little as two weeks from the time they ran away from home, involvement resulting from the predatory activity of exploiters. An inmate at Jackson State Prison, Michigan, testified that "generally what I and anyone else that you have seen getting models [for pornography] would look for would be someone that had a poor family background as far as a father image in the home. It was part of the whole picture. . . . There is no father there and the young model looks for a man who is his friend. The photographer, too, is a father substitute many times."[21]

Another inmate explained the involvement of youths in pornography by describing their desperate need for appreciation: "I have yet to see anybody who would get in front of a camera for money. . . . If [the models] haven't been appreciated by their parents. They would love to be appreciated by someone. So money is strictly secondary."[22]

However, other testimony emphasized that youth involvement was occasioned primarily by the survival needs of the exploited youths: "We know that many children involved in pornography and prostitution are runaways. That is not to say, of course that most are involved in these activities. Nevertheless it is clear that many of the children . . . paid by adults to perform sexual acts are homeless for all practical purposes. They resort to these activities because they have few alternatives for survival."[23]

On September 15, 1977, the committee filed a report on the hearings concerning S1585, the Protection of Children against Sexual Exploitation Act of 1977. The committee concluded:

> —That child pornography and child prostitution have become highly organized, multimillion dollar industries that operate on a nationwide scale.

—That the use of children as prostitutes or as the subjects of pornographic materials is very harmful to both the children and society as a whole.

—The committee has found a close connection between child pornography and the equally outrageous use of children as prostitutes.

—Who are these exploited children and how do the pornographers and prostitution organizers lure them into these activities . . . the child victims are typically runaways who come to the city with no money or only enough to sustain themselves for two or three days. It is estimated that 700,000 to one million children runaway from home each year so it is not difficult for pedophiles to find child models or prostitutes. Often adult exploiters pick them up at bus stations, hamburger stands and amusement arcades and offer them money, gifts, or drugs for sexual favors. With small children, even candy or a free meal may be sufficient.

—It should also be noted that at the present time federal obscenity laws deal only with the sale, distribution and importation of obscene materials. No federal laws deal directly with the abuse of children that is inherent to the production of such materials. It is the opinion of the Committee that such a federal law is urgently needed.[24]

On October 3, 1977, Congress amended and extended the Runaway Youth Act by enacting the Juvenile Justice Amendments of 1977 and added homeless youth to the categories of eligible recipients. This reflected an important realization that thousands of runaway youths were not simply capricious, but were indeed destitute. Congress also raised the amount of the grants from less than $75,000 to less than $100,000.[25]

Increased attention to males as victims of sexual abuse and the reported use of prepubescent children in sexual exploitation led to the report of the Committee of the Judiciary of the House of Representatives on October 12, 1977:

We agreed that the examples of child abuse, which involved transportation of young children for use as prostitutes were reprehensible and should be penalized. The committee also found some connection between child pornography and the prostituting of youths. Accordingly, the committee, upon the recommendation of the majority of our witnesses, reported our bill with a section that would amend the White Slave Traffic Act (commonly known as the Mann Act) to apply to minors. Present law only applies to females under 18.[26]

The issue of sexual exploitation of runaways continued to gain increased public attention. *Time* (November 28, 1977) reported that not only are runaways potential prostitutes, but that "typically they are the products of broken homes and brutality often inflicted by alcoholic and drug addicted parents. They take to the streets and use their bodies for survival."[27]

The 1978 murders by John Gacy of thirty-three young Chicago men ignited concern about individuals who prey on running and missing youth. In contrast to the 1967 *Newsweek* article that associated runaways with hippies was a 1979 *Newsweek* article about a runaway hotline. The article began as follows: "'Can I come home?' 'Yes. Absolutely. We can't wait. Thank God you are alright.'" and ended with a photo of a rain-drenched runaway captioned, "Are you Alive? Let Someone Know!"[28]

In 1980, Congress amended the 1974 runaway youth act to become Title III of the 1980 juvenile justice acts. This included recognition that services should be extended not only to homeless youths, but to their families as well. These expanded services would: (a) alleviate immediate problems of runaway and homeless youths; (b) reunite children with their families and encourage resolution of family problems through counseling; (c) strengthen family relationships and encourage stable living conditions; and (d) help youths decide on a course of action.[29]

As the services grew, so did knowledge about the nature and profile of runaway youths, about their numbers, about the seriousness of their home problems, and about the seriousness of the dangers and exploitation they are subject to while on the run. In 1980, the Senate Subcommittee on the Constitution estimated that there might be well over one million runaways, with 500,000 youths homeless! The Reverend Bruce Ritter, founder of Covenant House, at that time the largest runaway shelter in the United States, testified in 1981 before the Senate Subcommittee on Juvenile Justice and defined two categories of runaway youth: "The first category are younger children who run away from home to avoid situations of abuse and neglect, including sexual abuse. The second category, mostly older adolescents, may more properly be termed 'throwaways' instead of runaways as they have been forced to leave homes that can no longer sustain them."[30] Rev. Ritter argued that these youth are not just the prey of individual pornographers or other exploiters, but that "What we are up against, pure and simple, is the greed of organized crime which capitalizes on the disintegration of the American family by using children and young adults whom nobody wants to satisfy our society's most depraved sexual desires."[31]

The Department of Health and Human Services reported that in 1981 there were 169 shelters serving 45,000 youths out of an estimated one million runaways. It also noted that although the Runaway and Homeless Youth Act did not contain any specific references to juvenile prostitution, sexual abuse, or sexual exploitation of children or adolescents, the department had authorized research to "develop an indepth demographic and descriptive knowledge base on adolescent prostitution, with a special focus on juvenile males, and to determine the relatedness of this phenomena to youth involvement in pornography and to runaway behavior."[32] The department noted that "despite their differences, there are important similarities between adolescent male and female prostitutes, including socioeconomic backgrounds (many are middle class youths), race and ethnicity (primarily white), single parent or non-intact nuclear families, education and employment histories (both characterized by negative experiences and poor achievement), and extensive runaway histories or involvement with law enforcement agencies."[33]

Newsweek, October 18, 1982, reported these findings in an article entitled, "A Nation of Runaway Kids":

> A new generation of the American youngster is on the run, often at a desperate pace. They resemble less their romantic predecessors, from Huck Finn to the Flower children, than refugees fleeing the wreckage of their families. . . . Even if sufficient money could be found to put counselors on every street corner, more fundamental questions remain. One's own home is, after all, supposed to be the place where they have to take you in, no matter what; being forced to leave it can be the ultimate rejection.[34]

The Subcommittee on Civil and Constitutional Rights on November 18 and 30, 1981, heard high regional and national estimates of the numbers of runaway youth: "Each year in the United States, approximately two million children disappear. Of these: 1,850,000 are runaways, 100,000 are taken by a parent, and 50,000 simply disappear . . . 7,000 runaways are picked up by Florida law enforcement officers annually. This is out of an estimated 50,000 children who runaway or disappear each year in the State of Florida."[35] Not only were these numbers larger than previous estimates, but they linked the issue of runaway children with missing children.

This led to the 1982 missing children's act, which (a) required the entry of names of children missing for forty-eight hours into the FBI's national computer; (b) gave parents, legal guardians, and next of kin the right to enter the missing child's name if local officials did not make the entry; and (c) specified that information on unidentified bodies be put into a national information system.[36] This information from this act would lead to increased concern about the abuse of children by their parents, a concern reflected in testimony on child kidnapping heard by the Senate Subcommittee on Juvenile Justice (February 2, 1983, and May 25, 1983).[37,38]

On June 16, 1983, the House of Representatives conducted a hearing on the protection of children against sexual exploitation. Testimony based on a study of the psychosexual abuse of children, focusing on children involved in pornography, suggested that these children were typical of the runaway/prostitute, with the highest number of youths being throwaways rather than runaways and with more than 75 percent reporting sexual abuse in the family. Interestingly, 60 percent had made prior contact with mental health or social service organizations, which indicated that these youths had come to professional attention earlier, but the attention had been ineffective. The report concluded:

These youngsters appear to share more directly characteristics of the adult homeless population. These children who are more pushed out than runaway appear to be the "undocumented aliens" of the general population and will be the homeless adults of the future. Their distrust of system resources, their pronounced isolation and their vulnerability for exploitation and misuse is so severe that the likelihood of their being reabsorbed into the mainstream of American youth culture seems minimal.[39]

The 1984 annual report by the Department of Health and Human Services on the runaway and missing children's act noted that estimates of runaway youths ranged from 730,000 to 1.3 million and claimed that 500,000 of these youths were for all intents and purposes, homeless. The youths were divided into two different categories. Those in the first category were family oriented, were between ages nine and sixteen, and had a tendency to be referred by self or school. They attended school, lived with their parents, and had been involved in previous runaway episodes. Youths in the second subgroup were "independent oriented" with either no family or with a family that no longer offered viable living arrangements. It was noted that these two groups would require substantially different interventions.[40]

This report also noted the substantially increased services offered by runaway shelters. In fiscal year 1978, 28,539 youths were served in shelters. In fiscal year 1981, the last year covered by the report, 34,662 runaways were served in shelters. There were also adjustments reflected in the percentages of the subtypes served, with an increase in the numbers of those youths categorized as homeless:[41]

Category	Fiscal Year 1978	Fiscal Year 1981
Runaways	45.2%	40.2%
Homeless	27.6%	34.5%
Crisis/not runaway	19.3%	20.5%
Potential runaway	3.4%	4.5%
Other	4.5%	.3%

This change in the population was reflected in the reported figure that over 40 percent of the youths served by shelters in 1981 did not return to the same living situation they came from at time of intake.

Testimony from the National Network of Runaway and Youth Services, Inc. noted that in several specific states runaways had been turned away from shelters because of overcrowding. The current available bed space was nowhere near the total number of youths on the street:

This estimate indicates that the federal OHDS [Office of Human Development ment Services] shelters served no more than one in three and sheltered no more than one in twelve of the individual runaway and homeless youth actually identified and counted last year in this country. . . . Police and juvenile probation advised us that only one in four or one in five runaways they ever see is arrested, detained or officially counted. . . . Applied against even the most conservative number of counted youth identified above (558,662) these multipliers of four or six would mean that runaway and homeless youth exceed two million annually.[42]

This report proposed a far different definition of a runaway: "A runaway is a child who is most often thrown from his home or asked to leave his home by a very angry, a very depressed, a very drunk, [or] a very high on drugs parent who simply cannot cope with [his or her] own problem, and that these kids are forced out. It is very rare that these kids want to run. Most children want to go home. They are not carefree children."[43]

This theme is continued in the 1985 oversight hearings before the House Subcommittee on Human Resources on July 25, 1985. The committee chairman, Representative Dale Kilder, characterized runaway youths not as "running to but as running from" numerous forms of abuse and neglect.[44] The size of the problem continued to grow: 271 shelters now provided 60,500 youths with residential services, drop-in services aided 305,500, and hotline services were used by 250,000 youths. In spite of this increase, testimony again indicated that youths were turned away from shelters because of lack of room. The committee asked the question, Are most of America's missing children, in fact, runaway children?

A report by the National Network of Runaway Youth indicated that the predators from whom children were at risk existed not only in the streets, but also in the home. It posed the question, To whom do these children belong? If they do not belong on the streets, and if they cannot return home, where can they go?

Many of these children, however, are throwaways, young people who have been forced out of their homes because they were physically or sexually abused or victims of extreme neglect. Providers believe that a high percentage of these youth runaway because their families have become dysfunctional, that is, the family has such economic, marital, alcohol, or mental health problems that there has been a total breakdown between the youths and families resulting in a crisis situation. Finally, some of these youths are socially and emotionally troubled. They have experienced a series of personal failures with their schools, the law, finding a job, drug and alcohol abuse, and other adolescent situations. They see leaving as their way out. . . . Young people are running away from something rather than running to something. The mistaken public perception that runaway and homeless youth are on the streets because they are pursuing a carefree and rebellious lifestyle is rapidly dissolving. . . . In a perfect world, the obvious answer would be to reunite all these children with their families. Our world, however, is less than perfect. Many of these children have fled their families because of abuse, neglect or other serious family problems. For those youth to return to the same crisis situations would only lead to more problems.[45]

The history of runaway youth in the United States reveals an evolution in the understanding of the issue. Initially, runaway youths were understood as capricious and undisciplined urban nomads. This perception gave way to alarm as runaways came to be seen as at high risk from predators on the street. Finally came the realization that great risk exists not only on the streets, but also in the homes the youths run from. Runaway youths have been associated with delinquency, with physical and sexual abuse both in the home and on the street, and with the dangers of prostitution, drug abuse, pornography, and physical assault. Runaway youths are now seen as the victims of these offenses.

Youths Who Run Away: A New Study

Contemporary research has found that insight into the process of victimization can be gained by studying it from the viewpoint of the victim. With that orientation governing our work, we sought to examine the effects of running away from home on runaway youths. We elected to study, from the vantage point of the youth victims, their cognitive perceptions and emotional reactions to the event of running away from home, their perceptions of family and family influence in their lives, and the presence of any physical and sexual abuse in their backgrounds.

Study Description

From 1983 to 1986, a study undertaken for the U.S. Office of Juvenile Justice and Delinquency Prevention explored possible linkages between childhood sexual abuse, juvenile delinquency, and adult criminal activity. Three separate populations were examined: (1) child sexual abuse victims, (2) convicted sex offenders, and (3) juvenile runaways. Covenant House cosponsored the portion of the study that dealt with juvenile runaways, which forms the basis for this book. In a cooperative effort with Covenant House-Toronto (also known as Under-21 Toronto) a Canadian youth shelter, data were collected from 149 adolescents who entered the shelter. Under-21 Toronto is a crisis intervention center for runaway and homeless youths between the ages of sixteen and twenty-one. The center provides basic needs: twenty-four-hour shelter, food, clothing, tokens or bus fare, valid identification, professional counseling and social work service, health care, and legal services for residential and walk-in youths. In 1985, they received approximately 12,000 requests for help from 3,933 youths, whose average length of stay was seven days.

Between June and August 1984, staff counselors who were specially trained in the study's objectives and protocol recruited adolescents to volunteer for the study. These youths were recruited from a total Covenant House summer population of 818 youths. Adolescents excluded from the sample included subjects who could not read or understand English, who were noticeably on drugs or intoxicated, or who did not keep the scheduled appointments. A comparison of study subjects with the overall client population in terms of age, race, education, gender, and religion was performed by project and shelter staff and indicated that the sample was representative of the adolescents served at the Canadian sanctuary.

After obtaining consent to participate from the adolescents, the counselors administered a structured interview and a draw-a-person graphic task. Information on family structure and environment, reasons for running away from home, prior physical and sexual abuse, physical and emotional symptomatology, and prior delinquent activities was collected. The Piers-Harris self-concept scale and modified versions of scales of measurement for life events were administered, as were measurements of presumptive stress and coping behavior developed by the Langley Porter Institute.

That this study was undertaken with a population in Toronto, Canada, is important. Although running away from home is considered a status crime in the United States, in Toronto it is not recognized as an arrestable offense. Consequently, exploring relationships such as those between prior abuse and delinquent activities in this particular sample of runaways reduces a potential confounding effect.

Sample Characteristics

Of the 149 runaways in the sample, 63 percent were male and 37 percent were female. Runaways reported leaving home from 1 to 110 times (mean = 8.9 times). They first left home from as early as four years old to as late as nineteen years old. Almost half, or 46 percent, had left home more than three times. Twenty-eight percent of the runaways had been away from home for less than one month at the time of the interview, 45 percent between one month and one year, and 27 percent for over one year.

Ages ranged from 15–20 years old, with a mean of 17.9 years. The majority of the runaways, or 81 percent, were white, with blacks accounting for 9 percent and runaways of other racial groups making up the remaining 10 percent.

A large proportion of runaways reported physical and/or sexual abuse. An overwhelming majority, or 73 percent, reported having been physically beaten. Forty-three percent stated that being physically abused by the people they lived with was an important reason for their leaving home.

Forty percent reported having been attacked or raped in the past. Thirty-six percent reported having had sex against their will, 31 percent as having been sexually molested, and 19 percent as having been forced to observe pornographic films depicting sexual activity. Sexual abuse was considered present if the adolescent reported at least one of these last three items. Fifty-one percent of the runaways reported sexual abuse.

Of the 110 runaways who estimated their family/household income, 41 percent reported incomes higher than most people, 39 percent reported incomes about the same as others, and 20 percent reported incomes lower than most people. The percentage reporting higher than most people was consistent with the finding that 45 percent of families were supported by both mothers and fathers. Thirty-two percent were supported by fathers only, 15 percent by mothers only, and 7 percent by general relief. About one-fourth of the runaways did not, or would not, provide information about their parents' occupations. Because of this, social class background of the sample of runaways could not be reliably documented. Inability to collect data in this area is a problem that has been noted in other studies of runaways and is most likely related to the runaways' not wanting to be found. However, based on experience and other sources, shelter personnel judge their clients to be largely middle class.

Study Limitations

There were several limitations to the study. The sample is small and includes only officially recognized, self-reported runaways. Covenant House, the treatment agency that served as the data source, is a place of refuge to homeless youths between the ages of sixteen and twenty-one. Consequently, the sample consists exclusively of older adolescents.

The study is also limited by data missing for some questions. Questions relating to ongoing delinquent activities could not be asked, and indepth information on the nature and frequency of reported sexual abuse could not be obtained. These youths are self-referred to the program and are free to discharge themselves whenever they choose. Since the information was collected anonymously with no connection to clinical services, there was no assurance that the runaways would seek out counseling for issues arising from sensitive questions. Consequently, the information on the history of sexual abuse is limited to the presence or absence of such abuse. Caution should be used in generalizing any findings to the general runaway population in either Canada or the United States.

2
Running Away from Home: The Avoidant Path

R unning away from home is an unusual and rare life experience. The 1986 research of James Garbarino shows that no more than 12 percent of American youth run away from home for any length of time before the age of eighteen, with no more than 3 percent of American families experiencing a runaway event.[1]

Even a cursory examination of contemporary experience with runaways reveals that these youths are running from something, not running to something. Running away from home is not a normative, healthy, or productive phase of adolescent development; rather, it is a reactive, avoidant behavior of a small percentage—yet large number—of youths in our society, youths who are desperately fleeing a stressful environment. In running away from home, these youths may escape a difficult home situation, but they do so at the price of short-circuiting their own growth and ability to chart an effective future as a contributing member of society. Ill-equipped and unprepared to survive on their own, they form a tragic picture of homeless youths victimized through violent exploitation by the sex industry, the illegal drug industry, and other criminal activity. Speaking with these youths leaves one with the feeling of wasted potential and needlessly unhappy lives.

There are three major misconceptions about runaway youths that allow them to drift without attracting supportive attention and thereby to continue to be victimized by exploitative predators: (1) running away from home is occasionally part of the normal adolescent cycle of separation from home; (2) running away from home is indicative of a disobedient, troublesome youth who must assume full responsibility for leaving home; and (3) a youth who runs away from home for whatever reason should be able to survive on his/her own without responsible adult support and guidance.

Examination of our findings based on data from the 149 runaway youths in our study brings us to the conclusion that running away is a premature separation from home, is symptomatic of a family crisis that often can be abusive in nature, and is predictive of a troubled future with increased vulnerability to abuse for the runaway. In this chapter, we address the misconceptions about runaways by presenting a view of adolescent development that is predominantly family centered. Far from encouraging an isolated and early separation from home, normative adolescence is, we believe, a period when the youth and his/her family carefully prepare, over time, for a successful separation and positive future for the adolescent. Adolescence as period of development pertains not simply to the youth, but to the youth in concert with the family.

How, then, does a runaway episode occur? We present two typical case histories of runaways from our sample population, cases that show that the roots of a runaway episode are in a family crisis, which results in the youth either fleeing for safety or actively expelled from the family by parents.

Normative Adolescence

Adolescence is a period of human development. Like all human development, it occurs with both the progressive accumulation of behaviors and experiences (called *continuous*) and with the rapid, age-specific leaps and crests of newfound skills (called *discontinuous*). Continuous and discontinuous adolescent development occurs on a physical, intellectual, and social scale.

Physical adolescent development begins in puberty and ends with the completion of bone growth. Intellectual development encompasses the period wherein the child achieves the management of formal operations.[2] Social adolescent development takes place in the context of the formation of a person's identity in relationship to family and society and can be measured as that sociological period between pubescence and the termination of the legal restrictions on compulsory education, juvenile criminal proceedings, and child labor laws.[3]

Adolescent human development has many unique discontinuous tasks and objectives, while it solidifies many of the continuous developments already achieved:

> Adolescence, the final stage of childhood, recapitulates many of the developmental highlights of earlier years. Like infancy, adolescence is a period of rapid physical growth and major changes in bodily appearance. Like preschool years it is a time of considerably expanding social horizons and the emergence of marked personality differences. Like middle childhood it is marked by increasing liberation from family ties and a continuing shift from home-centered to peer group and community activities.[4]

The developments in this final stage of childhood have been related with great alarm. St. Augustine called these years the storms of youth, and subsequent astute observers of human behavior have described them as causing great disorder and disarray,[5] as an interruption of peaceful growth,[6] and as perilous: "[In] no other stage in the life cycle . . . are the promise of finding oneself and losing oneself so closely allied."[7]

We take the position that normative adolescent development, both continuous and discontinuous, takes place in a more evenhanded and progressive manner than commonly perceived. It is for the adolescent, as Erickson writes, " a progressive continuity between that which he has come to be during the long years of childhood and that which he promises to become in the anticipated future."[8] Furthermore, we believe that in Western society it is the family that is responsible for the successful experience of adolescence that prepares the growing person to assume the responsibilities and joys of adulthood. Adolescence represents a developmental period not only for the child involved, but also for the parents as caretakers of that child. The family is the place where physical, psychological, intellectual, and developmental changes occur and are mediated, understood, and mastered. The family is the crucible from which the adolescent emerges as an independent person: "The ways in which the adolescent approaches the developmental tasks of this age period and the degree of difficulty these tasks present and his relative success in mastering them will all be importantly affected by prior and continuing parent child relationships."[9]

Physical Development

A child does not become sexual with the onset of puberty; rather, puberty is one stage of a person's sexual and reproductive development.[10] Physical development in both females and males can take as many as four years from onset to completion. This growth occurs at uneven rates within the individual, causing a variety of discomforting changes. Within the same age group, individual physical developments are even more uneven, resulting in adolescents of the same chronological age experiencing different levels of physical development.[11]

These ongoing physical and sexual changes introduce the adolescent into new realms of psychological and sociological development. For example, in her review of the literature, Chillman notes that early maturation has direct implications for the social lives of adolescents, with early-maturing girls tending to suffer social handicaps at ages eleven or twelve, while early-maturing boys seem to have consistent social advantages, at least through high school. Adolescents must become reacquainted with the limitations and potentials of their changing bodies, become familiar with their reproductive and sexual capacities, attend to the impact of their sexual attractiveness, and learn to integrate their new adolescent sexuality with interpersonal relationships.[12]

Elkind and Weiner have stated that adolescents are confronted with three conflicts: (1) sexuality vs. security, (2) intimacy vs. sexuality, and (3) intimacy vs. security.[13] The conflict of sexuality vs. security pits the adolescent's need to explore developing physical sexuality against the need for emotional security (in other words, how the adolescent handles sexual urges safely). In intimacy vs. sexuality, adolescents must resolve the question of how they are to become friends with people they find sexually attractive and still be safe. Finally, in intimacy vs. security adolescents must confront their desires to be close and intimate with people outside of the family and their needs for safety; they must find intimacy without being hurt.

Adolescents also must deal with societal expectations concerning their sexuality expectations, that vary from the pseudomature view of adolescent sexuality espoused by media coverage to the denial of adolescent sexuality by adults. In these cases, "young people appear far more erotic and sexual than they actually are and . . . adult fantasies and anxieties about their probable sex behavior are overblown. Adults tend to view adolescents from their own mature level of sexual activity and response and find it hard to realize that adolescents are merely beginners at the art and expectancies of sexual intimacy."[14]

Intellectual Development and Formation of Identity

Adolescence is a period of new intellectual growth, described by Piaget as formal operations, or the ability to manipulate symbols with higher order symbols. Simile, allegory, and metaphor take on meaning for the first time in adolescence. Adolescents are able to think about thinking, and think about other people's thinking, for the first time. They are able to conceptualize and construct theories apart from the concrete realities around them.[15]

They do so, however, in a relatively egocentric way. Concerned essentially with themselves, adolescents create what Elkind calls an "imaginary audience" that believes that others think, fear, and judge in the same way the adolescents judge themselves.[16] Private thoughts are projected onto all others and then interpreted by the adolescent as being public information. Consequently, the adolescent believes himself or herself to be continually under the specter of public scrutiny and judgment that comes directly from his or her own harsh and private self-examination. Able to construct ideals and notice shortcomings, the adolescent is now also able to evaluate not only himself or herself, but also his or her parents, comparing them with an ideal perception of how parents should act. Further, the youth creates what Elkind terms a "personal fable," a belief in his or her own invulnerability and uniqueness born of the egocentric thought pattern.[17] This leads the adolescent to enormous risk taking.

With the onset of formal operations, the adolescent develops a personal, second-order symbol system, called a sense of identity. One goal of adolescence is to form from the mixture of experiences, talents, tendencies, and likes and dislikes (many of which are contradictory) a sense of identity based on "the accrued confidence that the inner sameness and continuity prepared in the past are matched by the sameness and continuity of one's meaning for others, as evidenced in the tangible promise of a career."[18]

The establishment of identity is a multifaceted project that enables the adolescent to act independently as an adult:

> If the adolescent is to become truly an adult and not just physically mature he must gradually achieve independence from his family and adjust to his sexual maturation, establish cooperative working relationships with his peers without being dominated by them, and decide and prepare for a meaningful vocation. In the process of meeting these challenges a young person must also gradually develop a philosophy of life, a view of the world and a set of guiding moral beliefs and standards that however simple are for him non-negotiable. A basic philosophy is essential in lending order and consistency to the many decisions the individual will have to take in a changing, seemingly chaotic world. Before the adolescent can successfully abandon the security of childhood dependence on others, he must have some idea of who he is, where he is going and what the possibilities are of him getting there.[19]

Individuation and Independence

For a person to be an independent yet relational human being, functioning independently yet part of family and society, is a goal of adolescence. The successful resolution of adolescence is a prerequisite to the growth and development that will occur in adult life. This successful individuation is the goal of both the adolescent and the goal of the parents: "The separation process can be conceived of as a gradually expanding spiral of mutual individuation and differentiation which increasingly leads to both parties (parents and adolescent) relative independence. This process lasts through a child's infancy, adolescence and early adulthood."[20]

Not surprisingly, completion of individuation in adolescence raises ambivalent feelings for both the parent and the adolescent. The adolescent is interested in exploring new physical, sexual, relational, and intellectual capacities, while parents look with pride at the achievements of their child. However, this exploration exposes the adolescent and his or her developing abilities to the possibility of failure and the personal responsibility for that failure. Earlier, parents have anticipated such failures, protected their child from them, and only gradually allowed the child to explore and to develop experience. In adolescence, the youth typically desires freedoms and eschews the responsibility that accompanies them. The youth continues to look to parents for protection but no longer is content to be protected in the same way as during childhood. Parents, for their part, must allow the adolescent to explore areas they have protected the child from. Although this may be frustrating, parents know that their role has been to prepare the adolescent for just such an independent exploration.

The adolescent is unsure of what it means to be an adult child of parents who are important to him or her, and parents are ambivalent about releasing a child to whom they devoted years of caring. The role confusion of a developing adolescent promotes a developmental crisis in parents as well. How much freedom they grant, how much protection they offer, how much failure they allow their child to experience are all issues parents must face daily. Furthermore, they must cope with the reality that the adolescent, while still deeply dependent on them for support and affection, also is turning to persons outside the family in demonstrating affections. They must prepare themselves for the time when the primary love and work objects of the child will be outside the family.

The resolution required for a successful transition by the adolescent entails continued parental support: "What he [the adolescent] most often needs is a graduated experience in autonomy in which his parents respect his capacities but stand ready to help and support him when he gets into situations he doesn't know how to handle."[21]

Individuation is a goal for the development of the adolescent and of the parents as adults and is achieved as a result of a partnership between adolescent and parent that alters the life roles of them both:

> Adolescents seek to become and to be recognized as individuals and in this drive they need to become distinct from the persons they were in the parent child relationship. However, since they have been formed through this relationship, a complete severance would undermine the self. Adolescents, therefore, also seek to remain connected to this relationship. As their movement towards individuality progresses, the old relationship becomes less suitable and the need for its revision becomes greater. The solution lies in transforming the relationship so that a balance is achieved between the two movements.[22]

Social Tasks of Adolescence

At the most primitive level, adolescents must be able to acquire enough basic skills in order to survive. At the very least they must have the ability to shelter, clothe, and feed themselves. They also must be able to engage in satisfying human relationships, with the goals on continuing their development as persons and of contributing to their society. These interpersonal and societal objectives do not take place within a vacuum. They are directly related to the history and society of the adolescents.

Prior to the period of 1880–1920, most parents put adolescents directly into the work force as soon as they were physically able to perform the work required.[23] It was not uncommon for marriages to be arranged by parents, and futures were charted based on the needs of the family.[24] The advent of the industrial age occasioned two factors that altered this pattern. First, with the industrialization, preparation for the future required education for economic success. Youths needed to be prepared for the work force with skills beyond those possessed by their parents. Thus, the entry of adolescents into the work force was delayed by an educational period. Parents began to devote themselves to the education of their children as the primary means of preparing for a successful individuation. Second, the works of Charles Dickens,[25] Upton Sinclair,[26] and others, describing the abuse of youths in industrialized places, engendered protection in the form of child labor laws, the development of a juvenile penal code and procedure different from that applied to adults, and the establishment of a form of compulsory education. These economic and humanitarian factors created an extended adolescence that focused more on development of the child than on apprenticeship to a skill.

What occurred then is what occurs now in the socialization of adolescents: "Adolescents and parents form an alliance designed to form an adaptive anchor to help adolescents meet the demands of society. The entrance of adolescents into society is made easier where their parents provide support and lay down guidelines."[27] This parent-child alliance that structures success for each developmental task appropriate to adolescence accounts for successful growth and a successful transition to the challenges germane to young adult life.

Summary

Michael Rutter summarizes the process of change in the successful normative adolescent period as follows:

> Certainly important changes take place but they are not usually accompanied by gross behavioral disruption or marked emotional dis-equilibrium. With all those bodily and social changes during the second decade of life one might expect more disturbances than actually occurs. There are three factors that are probably relevant to any explanation of why this does not happen in most individuals. Firstly, many of these changes represent increased capacities of various kinds; cognitive skills become both more complete and more flexible as powers of abstraction and logic makes new problem solving easier than it was when younger; social skills increase in range and complexity and the powers of love and friendship expand and mature; also emotional development includes an enhanced ability to appreciate other people's feelings and to understand their point of view. Secondly, substantial continuities of development are apparent. The crisis of adolescence are not wholly new and to a considerable extent the patterns of psychological functioning which emerges during the 'teens represent a growth and maturation of patterns already established in earlier childhood. The coping mechanisms developed when

younger in relation to other life crisis continue to have some relevance and the changes in adolescence build on what has gone before. Thirdly, not all the changes take place at the same time. Adolescence spans some half-dozen years or more and for most young people, puberty, the first love affair, critical school examinations, transition to employment, leaving the family and the various other life crisis do not coincide. Rather they come in series so that success in coping with the first gives both greater confidence and improved skills for dealing with the second.[28]

Adolescence, then, is indeed a task that faces not only the adolescent person, but also the parents of the adolescent. Together they build on the growth they have achieved; together they prepare for new roles as parents and children; together they struggle with the challenges of assuming those new roles.

Adolescents in Turmoil

Although successful adolescent development requires new roles from both parent and child and is often associated with stress and conflict, it is not usually pathological. Researchers suggest that about 20 percent of nonpatient adolescents report experiencing serious turmoil as they grow up; nevertheless, only 3 percent of American families report turmoil reaching the point of a youth's running away.[29,30]

How is the necessary alliance between youths and parents disrupted? Development psychologists believe that generational conflict takes place on a serious scale as a result of a serious breakdown in the family system: "The major source of issues for the generational conflict lies in the real or imagined violations of implicit contractual arrangements between parents and their children."[31]

The contractual agreements are either bargains (parents offer rewards or withhold punishment in return for a specific behavior), agreements (where both parents and child agree to abide by a set of rules over an extended period of time), or contracts (unspoken demands made by parents and child with one another). Through these contractual agreements, parents expect age-appropriate achievement and children expect material, intellectual, and emotional support. With the challenges of separation confronting adolescents and parents, the expectations of parents and support needs of adolescents intensify. *If these contracts are broken, the adolescent may feel unloved and rejected, the parent may feel betrayed, and the result may be that the adolescent either runs away from home or is expelled from the home prematurely.*

Flight from Home

Literature provides a classic example of the violation of the parent-child relationship. In Mark Twain's *The Adventures of Huckleberry Finn,* Huck is living with the Widow Douglas when his father, Pap, steals him away in the middle of the night and takes him to a deserted cabin:

> By and By pap got too handy with his hick'ry, and I couldn't stand it. I was all over welts. He got to going away too much, locking me in. Once he locked me in and was gone three days. It was dreadful lonesome. I judged he got drown, and I wasn't ever going to get out anymore. . . . I don't know how long I was asleep, but all of a sudden there was this awful scream and I was up. There was pap looking wild and skipping about every which way. . . . By and by he rolled out and jumped up on his feet looking wild, and he see me and he went for me. He chased me round and round the place with a clasp knife, calling me the Angel of Death, and saying he would kill me, and then I couldn't come for him no more. I begged, I told him I was only Huck; but he laughed such a screechy laugh, and roared and cussed, and kept on chasing me up. Once when I turned short and dodged under his arm he made a grab and got me by the jacket between my shoulders, and I thought I was gone; but I slid out of that jacket quick as lightening, and saved myself. Pretty soon he was all tired out, and dropped down with his back against the door, and said he would rest a minute and then kill me. He put his knife under him, and said he would sleep and get strong and then we would see who was who. So he dozed off pretty soon. By and By I got the old split bottom chair and clumb up as easily as I could, not to make any noise, and got down the gun. I slipped the ramrod down it to make sure it was loaded, and then laid it across the turnip barrel, pointing towards pap, and sat down behind it to wait for him to stir. And how slow and still did the time drag along.[32]

The next day, Huck escapes and runs for his life with the escaped slave Jim. Abduction, physical beating, isolation, alcoholism, and attempted murder define pap's parental relationship to his son, Huck, and provide Huck with ample reason to run away from a home where he was not cared for to the relatively safer uncertainties of life alone with strangers on the Mississippi.

A case example from the population of runaways in our study has remarkable similarities to the situation in *The Adventures of Huckleberry Finn.* It illustrates the broken contractual agreements (physical and psychological abuse) between parent and child that result in the youth's leaving home. Dan is a tall, blond white male. Twenty-one years old, he is articulate, responsive and appears intelligent. He dresses in the popular "punk" style. Dan has left home a total of four times, first at age sixteen, the last time when he was seventeen. He has been living outside of the home for four years and was receiving services at the runaway shelter at the time of the interview.

Dan describes his family as average and as having no money problems. When Dan first left home, both parents were present and his relationship with his mother was warm and close, while his relationship with his father was cold and distant. Both parents were still in the home when Dan last ran away, but his relationship with his mother had become cold and distant. Dan describes his relationship with his father as frozen.

Dan says his father is a daily alcoholic. His family was organized around denying the alcoholism, with Dan responsible for locating his father when he did not return home and for making sure his father was put to bed in his own bedroom and was fed the following morning. He remembers asking himself daily, "Is he going to come home drunk? Where am I going to find him? How am I going to get him home?"

This reversal of roles, with the child placed in the position of taking care of the parent, is the first indication of broken parent-child contracts. The stress and strain of this reversibility took its toll. Dan reports experiencing during childhood frequent headaches, nightmares, and chronic lying. He also fantasized, daydreamed, and felt lonely and nervous. From age fourteen through age fifteen, Dan suffered severe anxiety attacks and was taken to a physician for treatment. He reports that the physician told him not to hold in his feelings. However, when Dan confronted his father with his feelings about the alcoholism, things "got out of hand." Dan's father became verbally and physically violent; Dan discontinued efforts at sharing his feelings. The basic contract that the parent should be concerned about the child's physical and emotional well-being was ignored.

The following year, Dan began to run away in response to the pressures he felt brought about by his father's drinking. The first time he ran away from home, he told his parents that he was leaving and traveled by himself from Toronto to London, Ontario, to see his sister. He had no idea what he was going to do: "I didn't know what I wanted or needed to do. I hoped that I would scare them [his parents], shock them into reality." It is important to note that the purpose of the runaway incident was to attract the parents' attention to his distress. However, his sister convinced him to return home.

On his return, his family did not talk to him about what he had done, although he knew his parents were angry at him. "They never talked to you about anything; you were always kept hidden. They thought I couldn't understand, [but] I made a point of knowing things." It appears that all members of the family were engaged in a continuous denial of Dan's problems.

Other than running away, Dan reports limited delinquent activity. Only once did he take something from a store, break a window, and otherwise damage public property. He has "several times" smoked marijuana, been drunk, or used drugs other than marijuana or alcohol.

The next two episodes of running away from home were also related to the alcoholic behavior of Dan's father. As did the first episode, they lasted for periods of less than one week. Neither of these incidents mobilized the family around Dan's needs.

Dan's psychosexual development was associated with the fourth and final running incident. This time, his running away was occasioned by family problems related to Dan's disclosure that he was gay. This disclosure was a major violation of parental expectations for Dan's sexual development. Immediately after disclosure, Dan was sent to his sister's home. His mother told him that if he ever returned home, "your father will kill you."

Dan's childhood symptoms of distress, his anxiety attacks, his physician's medical advice, and his three earlier runaway incidents did not mobilize his family. However, his disclosure of sexual preference dominated family attention and resulted in a period of vigilance and restriction. After this disclosure, Dan's house keys were confiscated, his room searched, his telephone messages not relayed, and his letters opened. Dan perceived these attentions as major violations of the basic freedoms and privileges that he was accorded when he quietly took care of his alcoholic father.

This situation led to a final incident in which, after drinking, Dan's father picked Dan up by the hair, threw him against a wall, and chased him through the house with a butcher knife. Dan escaped by running into his bedroom and barricading the door. When he determined that his father had "passed out," Dan was able to make an escape.

The following day the family reacted as if nothing had happened. His mother "just passed it off." "You are some mother," Dan told her, enraged that there was no contract between himself and his mother that would protect him from life-threatening attacks by his father. Shortly after, Dan made plans to leave home. He saved money and took a bus to California, where he stayed for a year before returning to Canada.

This separation from home did not resolve Dan's problems. He still experiences some significant distress, reporting headaches, cutting or hurting himself, daydreaming, loneliness, depression, and suicidal feelings. In his four years away from home, he has encountered a series of survival problems: not being accepted; not having money; the dangers of hitchhiking; suffering from cold and exposure; and not knowing where he is going, how he is going to get there, or what he is going to do. He feels that he has trouble adjusting to independence.

While in California, Dan had a satisfying long-term relationship with a lover. Dan was nineteen years old; his lover was twenty. Despite this positive relationship, Dan left California with the feeling that he was unable to survive on his own. He reports "falling head over heels [in love]. . . . What does a beautiful Californian see in me, a hick from Canada? He still wants me, he wants me to come back. Six months ago I said no. [But] now [that] I am getting my life together, I plan to go back." When asked if there was anything in his life he would like to experience again, Dan replied, "The year I spent with my lover in California. I would love to have that again."

Dan has been in therapy for the past year. He believes that, as a result, he is somewhat satisfied with his sexuality. He reports positive feelings and perceptions of his self-worth and ability. Asked to describe himself, he says, "loving, caring, strong-willed survivor, pretty good guy." He likes his ability to learn quickly and to converse well, his artistic ability, his height, and his ability to interact with others. He dislikes certain physical attributes (chin, big feet, moles) and says what he needs most right now is "support, love, compassion, stability, and motivation."

In one month he hopes to be "in my own backyard . . . working, going to school." In five years he hopes to be in California, where he will be either a social worker or successfully in business for himself. He hopes that when he is forty he will be almost ready to retire and would like to own several successful businesses, have at least two houses and a car, and be happy.

Despite these typically age-appropriate goals, Dan is somewhat at a loss over how to address these goals and make preparations for his future by himself. He lacks several skills and abilities that would lay the groundwork for a successful future. Dan is faced with practical problems: no job skills, inadequate education, no entry into the workforce.

Dan's family relationships are unresolved. Although he has not seen his parents for over two years, Dan wishes that he could be together with them and that they would accept him. He conveys a deep sense of disappointment as he reflects that this will never happen. His response to the question, What would be different in the way you would treat your child from the way you have been treated by your parents?, reveals his perceptions of the broken parent-child contracts. "There would always be communication; [my children] could talk to me about anything. I wouldn't hide anything from them, I'd tell them everything that was going on, I'd treat [them] with respect all the time, [and] I'd give them every opportunity I could."

Dan's interpersonal relationships are in disarray, perhaps as a result of his inability to feel secure in himself. Dan has a longing for the relationship he had with his lover in California and now feels regret that he did not feel stable enough to maintain the relationship. He remembers the relationship as the one thing in his life he wishes he had again and now is trying to establish himself internally in order to return and resume the relationship. Dan's desire to overcome his lack of accomplishments and to prepare for his future is revealed when he remarks that at the end of his life the best thing he hopes people will say about him is, "We knew he could do it."

Dan represents the runaway whose family is so embroiled in an interpersonal crisis (alcoholism) that the needs of the youth are not only neglected, but the youth is assaulted if he does not meet the parents' needs. Dan avoids the tension and dangers of his family by running away. He is confronted by his attachment to his family and his inability to survive on his own and, thus, returns home. The family situation worsens; Dan runs away again, is confronted by the same problems, and returns yet again. It is only when the situation at home becomes dangerous that Dan realizes that no matter what the cost of leaving home, he has no option but to leave and struggle on his own.

Expulsion by Family

Dan is an example of an adolescent who flees from home for his sanity and, ultimately, his safety. Another type of runaway is the throwaway, the youth who is expelled from his family and then, alone and unprepared, must confront the dangers of the street. There is no family loyalty or bonding between parent and child. In this case, it is the parent who avoids the demands of the child's development to such an extent that the child is forced out of the house.

The most famous example of this situation is recounted in Charles Dickens's *David Copperfield*. David's devoted widowed mother falls under the spell of Mr. Murdstone, whom she marries and then allows to teach and discipline David. One day, Mr. Murdstone flogs David for failure in the school lessons he administers:

> He walked me up to my room slowly and gravely (I am certain that he had a delight in that formal parade of executing justice), and when we got there, suddenly twisted my head under his arm.
>
> "Mr. Murdstone! Sir!" I cried to him; "don't! pray don't beat me! I have tried to learn, sir; but I can't learn while you and Miss Murdstone are by I can't, indeed!"
>
> "Can't you indeed David?" he said. "We'll try that."
>
> He had my head in a vise; but I twined around him somehow, and stopped him for a moment, entreating him not to beat me. It was only for a moment that I stopped him, for he cut me heavily and instant afterwards; and in the same instant I caught his hand with which he held me in my mouth, between my teeth, and bit it through. It sets my teeth on edge to think of it.
>
> He beat me then as if he would have beaten me to death. Above all the noise we made, I heard them running up the stairs, and crying out. . . . Then he was gone, and the door was locked outside; and I was left lying, fevered, hot, and torn and sore, and raging in my puny way, upon the floor.
>
> How well I recollect, when I became quiet, what an unnatural stillness seemed to reign through the whole house! How well I remember, when my smart and passion began to cool, how wicked I began to feel!
>
> I sat listening for a long while, but there was not a sound. I crawled up from the floor, and saw my face in the glass, so swollen, red and ugly that it almost frightened me. My stripes were sore and stiff and made me cry afresh when I moved; but they were nothing to the guilt I felt. It lay heavier on my breast than if I had been a most atrocious criminal, I dare say!"[33]

After six days of solitary confinement in his room, David Copperfield is sent away from home forever, a decision made by Mr. Murdstone and acquiesced to by David's mother.

A similar case of an expelled child from our sample population is that of Dave, a nineteen-year-old, white male, 6 feet tall and weighing 170 pounds. He has brown curly hair, blue eyes, and a fair complexion.

Dave's early childhood was spent in Greece, where he lived with his parents until he was six. When he was six, his mother divorced and remarried within the same year. Dave has not seen his natural father since that time. He remembers traveling after his mother's remarriage throughout Europe: "My parents were hippies, into drugs and all that. We hitchhiked all over Europe, then went to Vancouver, came to Toronto in 1976, and became yuppies."

In Toronto, Dave's mother became a successful writer and editor, her work consuming large amounts of her time. Dave's relationship with his mother is not close. Dave recalls her seldom being home and feels he was essentially on his own. He describes his relationship to her as conflictual, seeing himself and his mother close only in times of conflict. Otherwise she was rather distant and unavailable on account of her work.

Dave states that he hated his stepfather, describing their relationship as cold and businesslike without any interpersonal qualities. Difficulties with his stepfather apparently began right after the man married Dave's mother. Dave reports that he was physically beaten when he was seven years old by his stepfather. During an argument at dinner the stepfather picked the boy up by his hair and threw him up the stairs. Physical confrontations continued. When he was ten, his stepfather punched him in the face because the boy forgot to pack a sleeping bag for a family holiday. Dave recalls that just before his second runaway incident, his stepfather pushed him against the wall and dared him to throw a punch, claiming, "When I was sixteen I scrapped with my father."

Not surprisingly, Dave showed physical and social symptoms of distress during his childhood. He experienced headaches, sleep problems, nightmares, shyness, cutting himself, chronic lying and fantasizing, daydreaming, feeling lonely, depression, nervousness, and fear of adult men. At thirteen, he began to use drugs himself and to sell drugs to children in the neighborhood. That same year he was sent to jail. "I got into a major fight. I slammed his head into the street. I don't know how I went out to inflict hurt."

Dave states the only reason important to his leaving home the first time (at age fifteen) is that he was thrown out by his mother. "We had a conflict about goals in life, [such as] school [and] work." Dave's mother and stepfather argued that Dave should have been out of the house "a long time ago." He is resentful that his mother never admitted that this was wrong. He returned home within a day or so, but problems in the home continued, with both Dave and his parents not living up to mutual expectations.

The first time he left home of his own volition was at age seventeen. "I up and went to Florida. I said, 'I'm going downstairs to do my homework' and didn't talk to them till I was down there [in Florida] and sent them a postcard saying, 'I'm having a great time, how are you guys doing?' That's how I am. I do things on impulse. I only thought *if* I could pull it off."

Dave returned home the first time because, "I was too inexperienced. I was getting into trouble in Ft. Lauderdale." When he first returned, his family's reaction was "cautiously quiet, they wanted to see what I was going to do. . . . They did nothing for me. I remember I got pissed off and said, 'You are supposed to be doing all of this!' but from then on I was not allowed to speak up to my mother."

When he returned home the next time, Dave's mother "reacted more harshly," concerned that he would influence his sister. Three or four months before he left home the last time, Dave's stepfather and mother split up, which he believes was directly related to tensions between himself and his mother. Dave describes his relationship with his mother prior to his leaving home the last time as "shaky, I knew it was coming, there were warning signs, feelings in the air. I started to think about what I was going to do, thinking of suicide and all that. She told me, 'I want you out by July 1.'"

Dave is ambivalent about returning home but thinks it would not be a good idea because "there would be more trouble." He still maintains contact with his sister, as well as his stepsister and stepfather. He and his stepfather commiserate about his mother. "He hates her as much as I do. After the divorce my stepfather said, don't lose touch. . . . He never sounded like that before." Although it appears Dave would like to see his stepfather on a regular basis, he has not taken steps to do so. In addition, he has not contacted his stepfather or any other member of his family for assistance while he has been on his own. He says that he "doesn't take up with mom anymore," and does not believe his mother cares if he ever comes back.

Leaving home has always been very difficult for Dave. Issues of survival and danger have been prominent in his history. The last time he left home, "I went up to a family cottage, got a job, went to another college, then got sick of it. I was broke. I came to the city, dealt drugs, got an apartment and student welfare ($375 per month), [and] stopped dealing drugs, but rent was $250 [and] that left $125 for food and everything else. I went back to Florida and then came back here. I was almost shot down there dealing drugs. Everything went bad. Even John Lennon got killed on my birthday."

Dave continues to show symptoms of distress. He currently experiences headaches and sleep problems, fantasizes a good deal, feels loneliness, experiences depression, reports suicidal ideation and nervousness, and is unsure how he feels about adult men. He lists his survival problems as being able to relate to friends and family and getting a good job and a good apartment. "It is not as easy as I make it sound. I don't show how I'm doing. You tell everyone that you have no problems. You don't know who you can trust, so that is what you say. I haven't had a foothold yet." He is aware that he has been the problem in meeting survival needs: "I'm lazy. I have trouble with money. I'd spend $300 for cocaine for one night and then think I could have had an apartment for a month." However, he feels that "now I'm a lot more intelligent about doing things the right way. I have so much more experience."

He describes himself by saying, "I'm a smart guy but when it comes to fun I'm not smart enough to make the right choice." He also relates that the best thing people could say about him is this: "He was the one to get the party going, the one to cheer people up when they were down, the one smiling face." Qualities he likes about himself are that he is intelligent, popular, spontaneous, trustworthy, and can get to the point. He does not like the fact that he can be irresponsible and uncommitted, has bad habits, is a coward and paranoid, and feels selfish. Dave says that he feels he is a person of equal worth, has a number of good qualities, is able to do things as well as others. Yet he also says he feels he is a failure, wishes he could have more respect for himself, feels useless at times, and occasionally feels no good at all. He shows a general indecisiveness and ambivalence when commenting about himself.

Dave expresses certain goals for himself. He wants to have a girlfriend, an apartment, a steady job, and a loving and understanding family. He says that in a month he will be doing well, but has no idea how this will occur. In five years he hopes to be back in school, but is making no plans to bring this about. He sees himself at forty in the United States or Great Britain, on his own and in business.

In responding to the question of how he sees himself as a parent with children of his own, Dave was very animated. As in Dan's case, the answers to this question shed light on what the youth feels he lost in his relationship with his own parents: "I'd love teaching [my children] anything and everything about life. Since thirteen or fourteen I've thought about this. When I was a kid if I did something wrong, [my parents] would do something wrong to me, get revenge. So I would be totally positive with my kids. I'd never hit my own kid. I'd always be around for my kid." When first asked if there was anything he would like to change in his life, he responded, "The whole thing." He continued, "Actually, one through eleven were okay; the last six to seven years I would have again, though, to do over."

Dave's manipulative delinquent activity, particularly selling drugs to others, can be typical of an expelled child:

> When the expelled adolescent separates he knows it is for him a matter of sinking or swimming. . . . He has been trained early to make it on his own. He has been trained to live in a human jungle where they try to outwit and manipulate each other, and where relationships are shallow and exploitative. In moving away from home early and moving into the peer group easily, he carries with him a world view and a style that may not appeal to many but they are the only ones he knows.[34]

Dave's early independence, lack of roots in early childhood, immediate conflict with his stepfather, and resulting conflict with his mother gradually increase. Feeling close to his mother only in times of conflict, it is not surprising that Dave creates so much conflict, demanding that his mother attend to him. Against this background, Dave has learned little about interpersonal relationships that is of use in making friends and committing himself to a career. His sense of failure and uselessness, coupled with his present depression and suicidal ideation, do not bode well for his future.

Psychodynamic theorists explain the intrapsychic conflicts resulting from premature separation in this manner:

> Being rejected and neglected by his parents, the expellee must seek his salvation in the peer group and outside world. He is pushed into premature autonomy . . . but shallow and attenuated, his relations with his parents are not devoid of conflict. In fact, conflicts with them can be hateful and cutting. This paradox is resolved when we realize that the attenuation of the parental bond does not only bring respite from massively reactivated oedipal and pre-oedipal entanglements; it also deprives the adolescent of the chance to grow through parent child conflicts and even more important, to grow through the experience of a tender and caring intimacy. This means he will lack those capacities and skills which thrive on caring, therefore his capacity to differentiate and perceive subtle feelings, to experience empathy, to delay gratification and to modulate and subordinate his own interpersonal behavior to long range goals remains blunted. Having lacked intimate and caring experiences with his parents, this adolescent's libidinal and aggressive drives are likely to break through abruptly and pre-emptorily making his attacks appear brutal or callous. This minimizes his chances for experiencing, even belatedly the kind of intimate and caring relationships he missed.[35]

Dave was neglected by his mother, abused by his stepfather, and, after he was expelled from his home, not only encountered more abuse, but learned to abuse others.

Arrested Development

For both Dan and Dave, their premature separation from home did not enable them to integrate successfully into society. Although Dan had been away from home for four years and Dave for one year at the time they were interviewed, they were, at that time, unable to provide themselves with basic food, clothing, and shelter. They both requested the assistance of an extensive shelter program. They both acknowledged that they lacked the requisite education and training to enter the job market. While they had idealistic visions for their futures, they had no concrete or specific plans for realizing their dreams.

The sense of identity is, as Erickson describes it, "the accrued confidence that the inner sameness and continuity prepared in the past are matched by the sameness and continuity of one's meaning for others, as evidenced in the tangible promise of a 'career.'"[36] According to this understanding, both young men have still failed to establish a solid sense of identity. With the assistance of psychotherapy, Dan appears to be more comfortable with his homosexuality than he once was. He also appears to be more convinced of his self-worth than does Dave, who reports his self-esteem in an ambivalent and contradictory manner. Both young men report many difficulties in establishing and maintaining interpersonal relationships, with neither one of them linked to relatives, friends, or lovers. Both find themselves concerned with their unfulfilled longings to have a successful relationship with their parents, and both doubt that will ever take place.

For Dan and Dave, an adolescence marked by familial abuse and absence failed to do more than provide the most rudimentary introduction to adult life. Few other tasks of adolescence were successfully completed. Excluded from the family system, the youths ran away from home, which accomplished nothing more than to enable them to avoid the most violent confrontations. Without the supportive guidance of family, their personal and societal development has been arrested and, perhaps, impaired. Consequently, their lives as adults has proved difficult and their prognosis problematic.

3
Families of Runaways

A ll human societies have primary groups that are responsible for socializing the very young. By chance alone, a child is born into a certain group of individuals with whom he or she will engage in frequent face-to-face interactions while learning to value these relationships, not as means to an end, but as ends in themselves. In these primary groups, commonly referred to as families, children first learn where they belong in society and what they can expect in life. For children sexually and/or physically abused by the members of their families, these lessons often impress on them that they are unwanted and unworthy individuals.

While conflict may be an inevitable part of all social interaction, including that which takes place in the family,[1] there is no doubt that family conflict is often destructive conflict.[2] It has a tendency to escalate—to increase in the number of participants, in intensity, and degree—and to become independent of its initial cause. Straus and colleagues estimate that in America parents kick, punch, or bite some 1.7 million children per year, beat up 460,000 to 750,000 more, and attack another 46,000 with knives or guns.[3] A recent nationwide poll reports that 27 percent of women and 16 percent of men were sexually molested as children.[4]

As more knowledge is gained about the effects of abusive family environments on children, it is becoming more evident that the ramifications are many. They may include displays of aggression,[5] delinquency,[6,7] anxiety and depression,[8] low self-concept,[9] running away,[10,11] and deviant criminal sexual activity.[12]

It is often hard to imagine, as well as to define, exactly what constitutes an abusive family environment. Is it one in which the physical punishment of a child "gets out of hand," where spankings become punches, kicks, and bites? One of the main problems with defining abuse, whether sexual or physical, is that abusive behavior runs on a continuum from what many might not define as abuse (spankings or siblings' "playing doctor") to behavior that leaves no doubt in anyone's mind (a father's raping or killing his child). However, after conducting an indepth interview with Pammy, one of the runaways in our study, we had no trouble determining that she had been both sexually and physically abused and that this abuse was the main reason for her running behavior.

Pammy is a good example of the type of chronic runaway discussed by Miller and associates in their study of street youth.[13] When the chronicity of running results from abusive treatment in the home, it signals that the child or adolescent does not have any other strategy for coping with or avoiding the abuse except to flee to the streets, to friends, or to another adult's protection.

While Pammy's case history may appear to be an extreme example of abusive family behavior, her case highlights several factors found in previous research to be associated with abusive family environments.: . . (1) the acceptance of physical punishment as an effective way to deal with childrens' behavioral problems, (2) family financial problems, (3) the presence of a parental lover or stepfather in the home, (4) abusive parental drinking patterns, (5) attitudes that condone deviant behaviors, and (6) the victim's fear of disclosure, which often ensures that the abusive experience is kept secret.[14–34] Our study of runaway adolescents also substantiated findings of greater verbal abuse and alcohol and drug misuse in the families of physically abused children.

A Chronic Runaway and Her Family

Pammy is a seventeen-year-old, white female, 5 feet, 7 inches tall and weighing 186 pounds, with closely cropped blond hair. She arrived for the interview talkative and friendly and laughed and joked about someone being interested in her experiences, although her laughter had a sharp, nervous edge.

Pammy has an attractive face despite a somewhat deep gash on her forehead. For the interview, she was dressed in what she generally prefers to wear—jeans and a sweatshirt. She said that when given a choice, she prefers sitting in a straight-backed chair because her legs were crushed by a tractor trailer truck when she was seven years old; as a result of the accident, she has two slipped discs and steel in her legs.

Pammy first ran away from home at age ten and has left home a total of twelve times. She last ran away from home at age fifteen and has lived on the streets, in shelters, in group homes, or with families for the last two years. Because she "failed at independent living," Pammy was back on the streets and arrived at the shelter the day before the interview.

Abuse History Prior to First Runaway Episode

Pammy first remembers her mother's living with a man named Hal. She is quite certain she was three at the time because at that age she fell asleep under a sandbox, and when she awoke she found that her mother had called the police and that Hal was among the "scared people all out looking for me." Hal continued as her mother's lover until Pammy was five years old. She remembers him best for being the first person she can recall who physically abused her. She was five years old at the time.

Pammy remembers that the incident started when Hal thought that she and her sisters had stolen $250 from him. When they denied it, he became angry and began to hit them. Pammy was hit over the head with a cutting board, hit around the neck with a horsewhip, and thrown into the fireplace. She remembers bleeding from her forehead.

Pammy also recalls that her mother was abusive during the same time period. Pammy related one such abusive incident in response to a question about her first sexual experience, rather than in response to questions about abuse. As she described this experience, Pammy displayed physical symptoms of extreme stress, including profuse sweating and shaking. She said that she had never before mentioned this experience to anyone.

When Pammy was five years old, her mother molested the child while bathing her. "I didn't know why my mother was feeling me up. . . . She was bathing me at the time. . . . I just cried. . . . I panicked. . . . She was drunk [and] came at me with a Coke bottle. . . . I felt the Coke bottle break." When asked why she didn't tell people at the hospital about what her mother did to her, Pammy says that she was scared and that she does not know what people were told. She thinks her brother made up something to tell people.

Pammy experienced two or three more beatings from Hal during the remaining few months before he left the family. For a short time after that, still during Pammy's fifth year there were other vaguely remembered men in her mother's life. Pammy recalls not wanting her mother to be with any of them. She bit one man on the leg, and he hit her for this. Also memorable for Pammy during her fifth year were her beginning piano lessons and a man named Harold moving in with the family.

Pammy describes Harold as being 6 feet, 4 inches tall and weighing 250 pounds. She recalls that both Harold and her mother drank all the time and that both were abusive to her and other family members. She recalls the first time that Harold sexually abused her; Pammy was seven years old at the time.

Pammy had gone to bed for the night and had fallen asleep after listening to Harold and her mother fight "about Mom's drinking. He screwed me; [it was] rape. . . . He must have walked into my room naked. . . . I had never seen a man all naked before." Pammy remembers screaming and that there was blood all over her bed. She also remembers not saying a word "out of fear." Harold continued to sexually abuse Pammy for four years.

The atmosphere of Pammy's early childhood development was characterized by sex and violence. Her sister became a prostitute. Pimps and prostitutes were close friends of the family. Pammy recalls one such friend who approached her several times to pose in the nude for him. Pammy, at seven, refused him every time and "took off in fear."

During the time from age five to age ten, Pammy experienced many incidents of both sexual and physical abuse by her mother and Harold. She recalls the first time that they physically abused her together; Pammy was eight years old at the time: "She threw me down the [cellar] stairs and I hit the cement [cellar] wall. When I came to, [Harold] hit me over the back with a two-by-four. Pammy can not remember why they did this, except that "both were drunk."

When Pammy was ten years old, her mother married Harold. Pammy says she was angry and upset over this. She describes her relationship to her mother and stepfather as cold and distant—"for the birds."

Pammy describes a highly distressed family life before she attempted to leave home for the first time. In addition to the constant abuse, family money problems were very bad—her stepfather, Harold, was in debt for about $10,000. She describes the way the family lived as marginal, but self-sufficient.

First Runaway Experience

When Pammy was ten years old, she got up one morning as if to go to school and, without mentioning anything to parents or friends, "just started walking." She had no specific plans and recalls thinking, "my feet will take me somewhere." She remembers being afraid of being kidnapped and trying to give the appearance that she had a destination. She wanted to "knock some sense into my parents."

Pammy says that her most important reasons for leaving home this first time were Harold's marrying her mother, her mother's and stepfather's alcoholism, and her being mentally, verbally, physically, and sexually abused. Around seven in the evening Pammy returned to her house and climbed into her stepfather's van to go to sleep, knowing that he would find her the next morning when he left for work. Pammy said that when she was found in the van, her mother was happy to see her and was worried that she was hurt. Her stepfather told her, "Pammy, I love you," for the first time in five years.

Continuing Runaway Episodes

Pammy continued to be sexually abused by her stepfather until she was eleven years old. The beatings by both her stepfather and mother continued until she was thirteen. During the period from age ten to her final departure at age fifteen, Pammy ran away from home eleven more times. Each time, except for the last, she returned home because "there was nowhere else." After the second time she left home, her parents stopped caring that she ran away: "They just didn't give a damn."

During this five-year period of running away and returning, Pammy became involved in various delinquent activities, including prostitution at age twelve. Her involvement was "not because I needed money . . . but because I wanted to get my parents' attention."

In the years before Pammy left home for the last time, her family environment was characterized by aggression and anger; family members kept their feelings to themselves and did not provide support for each other. Members were urged to be highly competitive, and family life was run by adherence to strict, inflexible rules. Pammy's parents continued their heavy drinking, and the atmosphere continued to be abusive. Just prior to Pammy's leaving home for the final time, her two-month-old sister was removed from the home by authorities because of parental neglect.

At the age of fifteen, Pammy ran to the home of a male friend, "another losing experience." She claims that the most important reasons for her leaving the last time were the sexual and physical abuse going on in the family and her parents' drinking. However, she also says that this time she left somewhat against her will, as her parents were "throwing me out anyway."

Present Feelings

Pammy has very low self-esteem. When asked to describe herself in a sentence, she says, "Ugh—I don't think too highly of myself." She does think that she has a number of good qualities—her personality, her eyes, the fact that she is tall and that she is able to defend herself—and that she is able to do things as well as most other people. She particularly prides herself on her musical ability. She can play the bagpipes (inherited from a grandfather), guitar, piano, organ, and recorder. She also speaks proudly of winning an award for singing in the sixth grade. However, she does not feel that she is as good as other people, she does not respect herself or feel that she has much to be proud of, and at times she feels useless and that she is no good at all.

Pammy says that she is angry with her parents and does not want to have any contact with them or return to the "hell" that she has experienced. She says that her parents do not care if she comes back and would not allow her to return, even if she wanted to do so.

Pammy reports suffering from headaches, dizzy spells, and sleep problems (nightmares), both in childhood and at present. She is lonely, "even if 150 people are around," and both likes and fears being alone, describing this loneliness as something she cannot deal with. She admits to self-mutilation, and when asked about suicidal feelings, she displays a multiscarred wrist (one scar still bright red) and says, "What do you think?"

Pammy says that she has never been cruel to animals or children, but admits to being assaultive to adults both during childhood and at present. She states that she has always been afraid of both men and women.

Pammy has never had an enjoyable long-term sexual experience. She is unsure of her sexuality, and although she is somewhat satisfied with it, she has confused feelings about it. She thinks of sexual activity as a form of violence, and although she constantly fantasizes about having sex, she is somewhat afraid of it and tends to avoid it.

When questioned about her plans for the future, this seventeen-year-old states that, depending on how things work out, she will either be back "working the streets," in a month or living in a Christian home and attending school. She has fallen behind in her schooling over the years and has only managed to finish through the ninth grade. Her ultimate goal is to work in missions, teaching people about God (she frequently attends church services), and to work in child care. Pammy is angry that she was forced to leave a group home at age sixteen, forced to leave friends and to try independent living. She says that she was not ready to leave. Her attempt at independent living failed, and Pammy wants to convince the people at the shelter to return her to a group home. She feels that probably will not happen, however, "because at seventeen I'm too old."

Parental Figures, Financial Problems, and Familial Abuse

As part of our analysis of the family situations of runaways, we took an indepth look at the interaction of parental figures present in the home and family financial problems in relation to physical and sexual abuse. We used only runaways who reported living with their families at the time of running (n = 90) and, because of the small number, excluded runaways who lived with one natural parent plus parental lover (n = 3).

We asked the runaways if a mother, father, or stepparent was present in the home and if the family was experiencing financial problems prior to their leaving. Of a total of eighty-seven families, 46 percent were intact (two natural parents present), 31 percent were headed by one parent (generally the mother), and 23 percent were reconstituted (one natural parent plus stepparent present). Approximately half, or 48 percent, of runaways reported running from a financially troubled home. Forty-four percent reported being sexually abused, and 35 percent reported that being physically abused in the family was an important reason for their running away.

We found that runaways from both intact and reconstituted families were more likely to report physical abuse in the family than were runaways from single-parent families (41% vs. 24%, and 37% vs. 24%, respectively). Physical punishment is still widely accepted as a way to maintain parental authority, and the male parent traditionally is in charge of this punishment. Our finding might be explained as resulting from the presence of a male parent in both the intact and reconstituted homes.

Examination of the relationship between parental figures present and physical abuse for families that were and were not experiencing financial problems showed that runaways from intact and reconstituted families were still more likely to report physical abuse than were runaways from single-parent families, regardless of financial status. However, this difference was greater for families with financial problems. Runaways from intact families and reconstituted families were much more likely to report physical abuse if their families were experiencing financial problems.

As Keniston points out, because most children now use the family income until age seventeen to twenty-five, the years of child rearing are the years of greatest financial stress on families.[35] Our findings suggest that a family's experiencing financial problems may serve as a stress factor that increases the risk of a child's being physically abused.

The relationship between parental figures present in the home and sexual abuse was also examined. We found that runaways from single-parent families were most likely to report sexual abuse (59%), followed by runaways from reconstituted families (50%), and runaways from intact families (30%).

Looking at the relationship between parental figures present and sexual abuse for families with and without financial problems, we found that runaways from single-parent families were much more likely to report sexual abuse than were runaways from reconstituted and intact families if their families were experiencing financial problems (81% vs. 43% and 81% vs. 50%, respectively). For runaways from families that were not experiencing financial difficulties, there was little difference in the reporting of sexual abuse for runaways from intact or single-parent families (21% vs. 27%). However, over two-thirds (67%) of runaways from reconstituted families reported sexual abuse.

A study of sexually abused children undertaken at Tufts New England Medical Center points to the importance of family financial stability and its interaction with the presence of certain parental figures.[36] Because single-parent families are more likely to experience financial difficulties than two-parent families, the researchers argue that single-parent families may move frequently and may rely on a variety of caretakers to provide intermittent help with their children. Both of these factors increase the likelihood of more people becoming involved in the children's lives, which provides greater opportunity for sexual abuse to occur. Our finding that there was no difference in the reporting of sexual abuse of youths from intact and single-parent families that were financially stable suggests that financial stability enables single parents to overcome many of the obstacles that confront single parents, including being able to provide adequate and safe care for their children during working hours.

Lifestyle factors that must be taken into account in any discussion of divorced and separated individuals are those related to the process of disengagement from an intimate relationship and the reinstatement of social ties. The disengagement-reinstatement process may, at face value, appear to be similar for men and women—both have suffered the disintegration of a crucial social bond, and both enter a gradual process of the reinstatement of social network organization. However, there are differences between men and women concerning what occurs during this gradual process. There exists a relatively well-defined set of expectations associated with the roles of wife and husband in our society, but with the dissolution of the marriage bond, this disappears. Instead, probably the most common expectation is that the individual will remarry or reinstate a social tie of an equivalent nature. This is especially true for women. A man may assume the role of bachelor, but the woman's assumption of this role is less socially acceptable.[37,38]

This social expectation has a greater impact on younger women and on those left caring for children from the former marriage, in particular those women who may not find themselves in the most promising of economic circumstances.[39,40] These women often have difficulty finding men to support them adequately because of their situations and because of the lower social acceptability of women marrying younger men. Pressured by societal expectations, these single parents often adopt lifestyles that put themselves and their children at risk.[41]

Children in single-parent families are often exposed to several new adult males to whom they are expected to relate in a trusting manner. This situation provides increased opportunity for sexual abuse of the child to occur. An adult male with a sexual preference for children may consciously select a single mother in order to act on his deviations, and many such men will marry the child's mother to guarantee access to the child.[42] Finkelhor reports that having a stepfather more than doubles a girl's vulnerability to sexual abuse—that this factor has the strongest correlation with victimization when all other background factors are taken into account and that "the high vulnerability of girls who have stepfathers is a function of both the presence of a stepfather and earlier exposure to a mother who was dating actively and may have put her daughter in jeopardy through the men she brought into the home."[43]

Our finding that a high proportion of reports of sexual abuse are associated with youths from reconstituted families was expected. However, we might expect to find runaways from financially troubled families reporting greater abuse. That runaways from financially untroubled families report greater abuse may mean that, given the tendency of many single parents to seek out a partner to improve the family financial situation, the new marriage partner is perpetuating the abuse.

Family Environments of Runaways

A 1984 study by Farber and associates of violence in the families of adolescent runaways who ran to youth shelters shows that 78 percent of the adolescents self-reported significant physical violence directed toward themselves by a parent in the one year prior to their running away.[44] These runaways, who ran from danger in their families, are typologized by Green and Esselstyn as "terrified" runners,[45] by Roberts as "endangered" runners,[46] and by Miller and colleagues as "victim" runners.[47] According to Miller and associates, victim runners are those most likely to be chronic runners:

> These youth feel their parents are their enemies and that to return home is to endanger their lives. While at home, the victims are possessed by an acute ambivalence; they fear their parents, see them as capricious and unjust, and yet at the same time they are dependent upon them, referring to them as a source of support and security. Once the underpinning of that support is torn asunder by some climactic episode, they confront the world as hapless and helpless vagabonds.[48]

The quality of the family environment is an important influence on the development of a child's self-concept, regardless of the type of family structure (i.e., single parent, two parents).[49,50] Family cohesion, when measured through the child's perception of family relationships, and family conflict are particularly important factors.[51,52] Further, the development of a poor self-concept is influenced by family conflict even when the conflict occurred several years earlier.[53,54]

Runaways have been described as having poor self-concepts and poor perceptions of their ability to exert control over their environment (e.g., to set realistic life goals guided by informed decision making).[55-57] These characteristics are indicative of poor social and psychological adjustment and decrease the youth's ability to cope constructively with stressors encountered both before and after leaving home.

In our study, we explored how runaways perceived their family environments by measuring ten dimensions of these environments and relating these dimensions to physical abuse and to the self-concepts of youths who leave home prematurely. The family environments of runaways who cite physical abuse as an important reason for leaving home (victim runners) are compared with those of runaways who do not cite physical abuse as an important reason (nonvictim runners).

How runaways perceived their family environments was addressed by use of the family environment scale (FES).[58] The FES is an individually administered, ninety-item, written self-report instrument that measures the perceived internal environment of a family.

Profile of Family Environments

Figure 3–1 presents a profile of the perceived family environments of our sample of runaways. Runaways who responded to questions on the FES

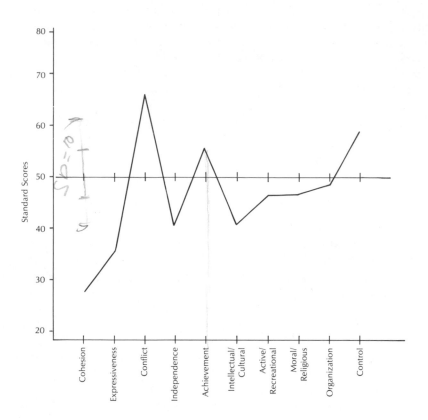

Figure 3–1. Family Social Environment Profile for Runaways

(n = 140) are compared to a national normative sample of 1,125 families. Illustrative profiles are plotted in standard scores with a mean of 50 (the mean of the normative sample) and a standard deviation of 10.[59]

Three dimensions of the family environment (cohesion, expressiveness, and conflict) indicate the quality of family relationships. Questions in this area are about such things as the degree of help, support, time, and attention available in the family, about how members express their personal feelings and problems, and about the degree of open and spontaneous discussion. As is shown in figure 3–1, runaways' families are less likely than are "normal" families to have members who are encouraged to act openly or to express their feelings in a manner that provides support. Instead, runaways perceive their families as displaying a high degree of openly expressed anger, aggression, and conflict.

The next five dimensions (independence, achievement, intellectual/ cultural, active/recreational and moral/religious) indicate the personal growth goals toward which the family is oriented; the last two dimensions (organization and control) indicate the degree of family structure or system maintenance. Questions in the area of independence ask to what extent members are encouraged to think things out or to act on their own—to stand up for themselves and their rights. Results show that families of runaways are less likely than normal families to have members who are self-sufficient or who make their own decisions.

Questions in the area of achievement tap the extent to which school or work activities are cast into a competitive framework—how hard members are pushed to be competitive. The families of runaways score higher than average on this dimension. This high score on achievement and the low score on independence are more important when the higher-than-average score on control (the last dimension on the figure) is considered. Questions in the area of control tap the extent to which rigid, inflexible rules are used to run family life. The higher-than-average family orientation toward achievement and control in combination with the lower orientation toward independence suggests that runaways' families emphasized achievement through conformity to rigid rules rather than through independence.[60]

Questions in the intellectual/cultural and active/recreational dimensions measured the extent to which family members took part in political, intellectual, and cultural activities as well as in social and recreational activities. These dimensions are believed to reflect facilitation or hindrance in social-skill modeling.[61] As shown, runaways' families scored lower than average on these dimensions.

As Penk and associates point out in their study of families of heroin users, the combination of above-average family emphasis on achievement by conformity to rigid rules and inadequate modeling of social skills suggests that the family experiences of runaways occur in an atmosphere of high expectation but inadequate preparation to meet excessive demands.[62] The heightened achievement expectations occur in the absence of the skills necessary to actualize these achievement goals.

Family Environment and Self-Concept

We related the ten dimensions of family environment to the self-concepts (or self-esteem) of runaways. To measure self-concept, we used the Piers-Harris self-concept scale, an eighty-item instrument with known reliability and validity.[63]

The results suggest that poor self-concepts found among runaways may result, in particular, from the low cohesion and lack of expressiveness in family relationships that exist in an atmosphere of conflict. The perception of runaways that they are inadequate in controlling their environment may result from their families' emphasizing achievement and mastery over the environment by conformity to rigid rules rather than encouraging independence and supplying necessary social skills.

Family Environment and Physical Abuse

We next asked the runaways if being physically abused in the family was an important reason for their running away. Of the 135 runaways who responded to this question, 43 percent said that physical abuse was an important reason. We categorized these runaways as victim runaways, with the 57 percent who said that physical abuse was not an important reason for leaving classified as nonvictim runaways. Because of the wording of the question about physical abuse, we cannot be certain that nonvictims were *not* physically abused. We only know that, if abused, these runaways did not consider the abuse an important reason for running away. We also do not know how many of the nonvictims may have left home because of other types of abuse, including sexual abuse. Both clinical and empirical studies show that there is a similarity between the home situations of children who are physically abused and those who are sexually abused.[64,65] Consequently, the fact that some of the subjects placed in the nonvictim group may actually belong in the victim group is taken into account in the interpretation of the results. These two groups of runaways were then compared on the basis of the ten subscales of the FES.

Illustrative profiles of the family social environments of victim and nonvictim runaways are shown in figure 3–2. Profile scores differ significantly for all but two dimensions. Most noticeable in the area of quality of family relations is that for victim runaways, cohesion or support among family members is almost nonexistent and expressiveness is low. As expected, conflict, or the open expression of anger and aggression, is higher for victims than for nonvictims.

The family orientation toward achievement through conformity to rigid rules rather than through independence is more marked in the profile of victims, although the emphasis on achievement is similar for both groups. It should be noted that the high level of expectations demanded by these families is a pattern commonly found in cases of child abuse. Some experts say that it is when the child fails to meet parental expectations that he or she becomes the focus of family violence: "Achievement is not encouraged to promote self esteem but to protect the family from an unacceptable image or from uncontrollable rage."[66] Gelles and Cornell also note the unrealistically high expectations that abusive parents have for their children: "It is not uncommon for a six-month old infant to be admitted into a hospital for injuries inflicted by a parent who was angry because the child was not toilet trained."[67]

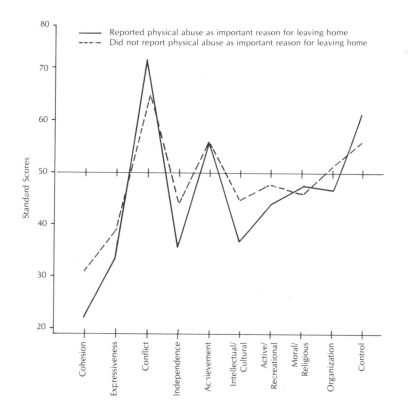

Figure 3–2. Family Social Environment Profile for Runaways Who Did and Who Did Not Report Physical Abuse

The victim group scored lower on the dimensions of intellectual/cultural activities and active/recreational activities. The finding suggests that this group, in particular, suffers from inadequate modeling of social skills.

Physically abused runaways, as expected, have an overall lower self-esteem than other runaways. They show a general dissatisfaction with life and a longing for things to be different. Indeed, only 50 percent of the run-aways who were physically abused in their families could remember their families as having been happy for more than three days.

The results of our analysis of the family environments of runaways provide evidence of highly distressed families, as perceived by the youths who left these environments. The findings suggest that runaways' perceptions of the quality of family interaction is related to running behavior and to the development of the poor self-concepts that runaways hold. They further suggest that runaways' feelings of inadequacy in exerting control over their environments result from characteristics of their childhood family environments. Both poor self-concept and inadequate coping ability increase the vulnerability of youths trying to survive in unprotected environments. Victim runaways, children and adolescents who run to escape danger in their families, are particularly vulnerable.

A Final Word

The results of our study show that the intrafamilial social support system in runaways' families is dysfunctional. This suggests that these families may be unable to cope with the running away experience and may be unable to adapt to the child's return to the home environment. Consequently, the return of the runaway to such families may only serve to exacerbate existing family tensions and to put the child or adolescent at risk for abuse.

The family dysfunctions revealed in our study are neither simple communication problems nor representative of normative adolescent separation issues. They represent serious dysfunctions, including physical and sexual abuse, that produce arrested psychosocial development in the youths and precipitate runaway behavior that prematurely introduces deficient youths to adult responsibilities. Thus, a treatment goal of simply returning runaways to such families is contraindicated. Unfortunately, as Miller and colleagues point out, most social and legal agencies that deal with runaways adhere to conventional detention and return policies—policies that merely set the stage for a repeat of the running episode.[68] One possible reason for agency and legal personnel adhering to these policies may be the belief that runaways are exaggerating their family situations. However, at least one study of runaways, nonrunaways, and their parents has indicated that parents of runaways tend to deny family conflict and to blame the child for running away.[69]

4
Social and
Psychological Outcomes

Historically, there are three noted etiologies for running away behavior. These are (1) the individual psychopathology of the runaway, (2) the pathological environment and social structure, and (3) the sociopsychological interplay between individual personality and social environment.

The traditional belief that runaway behavior originates in personal pathology is documented by the American Psychiatric Association's inclusion of the diagnostic category *runaway reaction* in an earlier version of its *Diagnostic and Statistical Manual for Mental Disorders*.[1] It now identifies runaway behavior as a component of a personal conduct disorder (i.e., undersocialized nonaggressive).[2] According to Brennan and colleagues, this belief about motivation for running away is supported by an accumulation of clinical evidence, gathered mainly by psychiatrists, counselors, and psychologists, that clearly places the cause within the individual youth.[3] The bulk of this evidence is the varied symptomatology found to be overrepresented in runaway youth, symptoms that include depression, loneliness, low self-esteem, lack of internal impulse control, delinquent tendencies, and subsequent delinquent activities. The runaway is seen as pathological and delinquent, and advocates of this perspective suggest policy that focuses on providing treatment for the individual, usually via counseling.

Opposed to motivational theories of individual psychopathology and receiving much support in the literature are theories that place the "blame" for runaway behavior on social-structural and environmental factors, including cruel and abusive parents. Advocates of this position believe that it is reasonable to expect youths to try to escape from these environments. The runaway is seen as not pathological and as generally not delinquent. Such a perspective suggests policy that focuses on providing treatment to modify the abusive environment rather than the runaway: "Advocates of this position would tend to scorn the suggestion that the child should receive psychotherapy or should be treated in any way. . . . Persons holding the social-structural perspective are usually strong advocates of the rights of youth and often work closely in direct contact with runaway youth."[4]

A third perspective on motivation is sociopsychological, a more complex perspective and one that is less frequently adopted.[5] Here, an attempt is made to synthesize psychopathology and social-structural approaches by focusing on an interaction between certain social conditions and the individual personality of the youth. Thus, policy associated with this perspective suggests that treatment must take both runaway and environment into account.

The sociopsychological explanation appears most congruent with the findings from our sample of runaway youths. On one hand, running away from aversive and abusive family situations is not only an acceptable, but perhaps also a healthy response on the part of these youths. On the other hand, our findings show that after the youths have left the home environment, they are highly stressed and participate in delinquent activities. Leaving the stressful family situation does not result in a reduction of stress, but rather in the presentation of seemingly pathological behaviors. We suggest that symptomatology traditionally associated with runaway youths and present in the runaways in our study is a stress response to an abusive environment, first at home, and then on the street. We propose that their delinquent activities are a maladaptive strategy employed to survive the hostile and abusive environment of the street.

In this chapter, we analyze symptoms associated with runaway youth and detail three specific constellations of symptoms: (1) post-traumatic stress disorder in physically abused runaways, (2) delinquency patterns in runaways and, (3) the silent reaction to sexual assault in male runaways. We represent these groups of symptoms as resulting from interactions between the individual psychopathology of the youths and the abusive environments that confronts them.

Response to Abuse

One Runaway's Experience

Marie is a sixteen-year-old, black female; 5 feet, 5 inches tall and weighing 110 pounds; with black, curly hair and a pretty, if overly made-up face. At the beginning of the interview, Marie appeared shy and nervous. She rarely raised her eyes; she spoke in a quiet, somewhat mumbled voice, and she twisted two fingers of her left hand with her right hand.

Marie first ran away from home at age fifteen and has run away twice. She last left home about a month before our interview and has been on her own for the last week.

The earliest that Marie remembers being physically abused is at age six. She says that both her mother and her father beat her at that time. When asked to recall that specific first instance, Marie is unable to do so and says that she thinks she was beaten because she did not do her chores. She recalls that her brother was being hit with a stick and dragged down stairs, and she remembers knowing she was hurt. Marie explains that she has trouble remembering things, as there were so many incidents that she cannot separate them. She was beaten every day that she can remember until she ran away from home.

When questioned about whether she had ever been sexually abused, Marie initially said she had not. However, during the discussions of her relationship with her father, it becomes apparent that her father molested her frequently, often during the physical beatings. Marie remembers his "always pinching my buttocks and touching my breasts." She says that her grandmother once told her that her father had raped his sister and that Marie should try to stay away from him.

When Marie was fifteen years old, she told her friends that she could not stand it anymore and that she was leaving. Without saying anything to her parents, she left for a babysitting job, called a girlfriend, and after getting permission from her girlfriend's parents, took a bus to her friend's home. She says that being physically abused was the most important reason for running away.

Her girlfriend's parents called the Children's Aid Society, and Marie told them about the abuse. She said that "they didn't believe me" and that they brought her back home. Her parents were angry with her when she returned home because "I left and because they said I made up stories."

The parental physical abuse continued during her final year at home, and when she could stand it no longer, Marie ran again to the same girlfriend's home. Her father and mother, when contacted by her girlfriend's parents, were angry. Sometime in the next few weeks her mother told her father that Marie was sleeping with a boy at the girlfriend's home. The father became enraged, went to the friend's home, and beat Marie. He "grabbed me by the breasts and threw me into a chair and then a wall." Marie ran away from her friend's home and traveled from her province to Toronto. Marie had arrived at the shelter the day before our interview.

Marie reports suffering from headaches, dizzy spells, and sleep problems (nightmares) during childhood and at present. She has always felt lonely and has always been afraid of adult men and women. She admits to shyness, nervousness, self-mutilation, and suicidal feelings.

Victim Reactions

A review of the general literature on abuse, sexual abuse in particular, shows increasing focus on victim reactions manifested in both psychological and social functioning. Anxiety about sexuality, guilt, sexual dysfunction, confusion, and fears have been found to be associated with prior abuse. For some victims, these reactions are accompanied by flashbacks to the victimization.[6-11]

Abuse has also been found to create subsequent difficulties in interpersonal relationships with individuals of both sexes.[12-15] Mistrust, arising from earlier victimization, may serve as a barrier to the forming of subsequent relationships or to the maintenance of relationships already in existence. Of primary importance in the adolescent stage of development are difficulties encountered in the formation and maintenance of peer relationships.[16,17]

In our study of runaways, we substantiated many of these research findings. Marie shares with Pammy and Dave, the runaways introduced in preceding chapters, a childhood history of repeated abuse. While these youths differ in the chronicity of running away (Pammy left home twelve times, Dave left three times, and Marie ran away twice), they share similar childhood and adolescent symptomatology, including loneliness, headaches, sleep problems, and suicidal feelings. We found that victims of familial abuse were more likely to report symptomatology indicative of poor social and psychological functioning.

In an extensive discussion of victim reaction to rape, Burgess documents the relationship of rape trauma syndrome to the official diagnostic nomenclature *post-traumatic stress disorder* in the *Diagnostic and Statistical Manual for Mental Disorders*.[18] She argues that identification of this pattern of victim response to rape is, in part, responsible for the contemporary view of rape as an event imposed upon the victim from the outside (i.e., as an external event), as opposed to the traditional view of rape as victim provoked.[19]

In a model of human response to severe stress, Symonds describes four phases of response in victims of violence. Phases 1 and 2 occur during the victimization, and Phases 3 and 4 occur in the posttrauma phase. Phase 1 includes reactions of shock, disbelief, and denial along with temporary paralysis of action and denial of sensory impression. Phase 2, or when denial is overwhelmed by reality, is termed *frozen fright* and includes terror-induced, pseudocalm, detached behavior. After the event (phase 3) the victim experiences circular bouts of apathy, resignation, anger, resentment, rage, insomnia, startle reactions, and a replay of the traumatic event through dreams and nightmares. The fourth phase includes restoration, resolution, and integration of the experience into the victim's behavior and lifestyle.[20]

Familial Abuse and Post-Traumatic Stress Disorder

The results of our study show that the symptomatology reported by runaway victims of familial abuse was consistent with the diagnostic criteria of post-traumatic stress disorder within the major category of *anxiety disorders*.[21] The four criteria include the following:

1. The stressor must be of significant magnitude to evoke distinguishable symptoms in almost everyone (e.g., rape or assault). Although the stressor under review is familial abuse, we must keep in mind that the very act of running away from home can also be defined as a stressor capable of inducing a significant stress response in an adolescent. Thus, the running episode serves to compound the stressful event for victims of abuse by family members.

2. The victim reexperiences the trauma, which is most frequently evidenced by recurrent and intrusive recollections of the event. Dreams and nightmares are common and very upsetting. According to Horowitz, this intrusive, repetitive tendency indicates that the event has been incompletely processed cognitively and thereby remains in active memory storage as a potential influence of behavior.[22]

3. The victim experiences a numbing of responsiveness to or reduced involvement with the environment. This psychic numbing may be observed through the victim's reduced interest in former activities or feelings of detachment or estrangement from others. Victims may be immobilized and refuse to venture outside.

4. The victim experiences at least two of the following symptoms that were not present prior to victimization: exaggerated startle response or hyper-alertness; disturbance in sleep pattern; guilt about surviving or about behavior required for survival; impairment of memory and/or power of concentration; avoidance of activities that arouse recollection; and increased reactions to other events that symbolize or resemble the traumatic event.

As table 4–1 shows, runaway victims of familial physical abuse appear to be haunted by their strong feelings about their running away experience. They are more likely than those youths who did not run away because of physical abuse to respond positively to questioning about reexperiencing the event of running away. They think about it when they do not mean to. ("[The] event kept popping into my mind."), and because of this they had trouble doing other things, including falling or staying asleep ("I had dreams about it.").

In our study, runaway victims of familial physical abuse are more likely to respond positively to items that indicate reduced involvement with the external world. They are more likely to report being afraid to go outside, feeling lonely, and withdrawing from friends. They report feeling afraid of having sex and of adult men. Indeed, they feel that they are "blanking" or "tuning out."

When other symptoms are taken into account, runaway victims of familial physical abuse differ most sharply in reporting headaches and sleep prob-

Table 4–1
Symptoms of Post-Traumatic Stress Disorder in Physically Abused
and Nonphysically Abused Runaways
(*percents*)

	Familial Physical Abuse	
Symptom	Yes (n = 58)	No (n = 76)
Reexperiencing of event (running away)		
I thought about it when I didn't mean to	55	45
I had trouble doing other things because the event kept coming into my mind	62	45*
I had trouble falling or staying asleep because I was thinking about it	52	38
I had strong feelings about it	83	69
I had dreams about it	53	32**
I couldn't believe it had happened to me	66	41**
Pictures of the event kept popping into my mind	72	49**
Reduced involvement with external world		
Feeling afraid to go outside	29	10**
Blanking or tuning out	64	45**
Feeling lonely	81	60**
Withdrawing from friends	56	46
Feeling afraid of having sex	28	14*
Feeling afraid of adult men	35	21*
Other symptoms		
Headaches	64	35***
Feeling afraid of being alone	58	32**
Crying	45	35
Feeling suicidal	52	42
Sleep problems	76	40***
Flashbacks	72	53*
Feeling like going crazy	55	31**
Feeling down on self	78	57**
Feeling unattractive, ugly	45	33

*$p < .05$
**$p < .01$
***$p < .001$

lems—probably related to their experiencing flashbacks. They are more likely to report crying and feeling that they are going crazy. They report feeling down on themselves and feeling unattractive and ugly. Not surprisingly, victims of familial physical abuse are also somewhat more likely to report suicidal feelings.

The results of our study indicate that post-traumatic stress disorder is a potential outcome for a large proportion of runaways, particularly for those who have been abused by members of their families. We also found that this diagnosis applies to both male and female runaways.

Delinquency among Runaways

Perhaps one of the most speculated about relationships is that between abuse, particularly sexual abuse, and delinquent/criminal activities.[23] A relationship between child maltreatment and delinquency, prostitution, and substance abuse has been described in the literature.[24-35] One study of an intact sample of moderately delinquent female adolescents finds a high (50%) incidence of sexual abuse, suggesting that this abuse may characterize the target population of delinquent females.[36]

In the United States, running away from home is classified as a status offense (as are such activities as gambling, prostitution, and loan sharking). A status offense is an offense that qualifies as a crime for an individual who is not yet legally defined as an adult. Although most crimes are seen as having both perpetrators and victims, running away from home is classified as a victimless crime (i.e., no one is considered the victim).[37] Instead, running away from home is seen as an act that violates those laws that enforce the moral code of our society: "The behavior is criminalized because society, or powerful groups within a society, define the behavior as immoral."[38]

This position is challenged, however, by the hypothesis that some running away behavior is a reaction to victimization. If delinquency and running away are closely associated, then perhaps the delinquent behavior, in addition to being a strategy for survival, may be tied to the runaway's experience of victimization.

Case Histories

Marie. Carrying a concealed knife for protection, Marie has used drugs other than marijuana and has gotten into one fistfight with another girl. She says that she did not fight back well, but now "I don't want to hold back anymore." She says that her brief time on the street has made her tougher. She is glad, but also frightened, of this. She finds particularly frightening the stories she has heard of lesbians, pimps, and prostitutes.

Dave. The last time Dave left home (at age eighteen), he got a job and went to another college before coming to the city and starting to deal drugs. Eventually Dave got an apartment, began receiving student welfare, and stopped dealing drugs. However, he still found himself short of money. "I went back to Florida and then came back here. . . . I was almost shot down there dealing drugs. . . . Everything went bad."

Pammy. According to Pammy, the hardest thing about being on her own is being alone and not having money. Dangers include never knowing who will knock on her door or harrass her. Pammy is especially afraid of pimps. She recalls that while living in a group home two years ago, some pimps armed with shotguns pulled up in a white limousine, "looking for some girls who screwed them," and waited outside for four hours.

For protection, Pammy carries homemade street weapons. She says she is proficient in karate, although she only uses it for show. She claims to be well trained in the use of a shotgun and has one at home that belonged to her mother. She needs to wait until she is old enough for a permit in order to use the gun. Her expertise with firearms is a result of spending a few summers at a camp when she was younger.

When asked about purposefully engaging in delinquent or criminal activities while away from her family, Pammy admits that several times she has stolen things from stores, taken cars for rides without permission, gotten into fistfights, carried concealed weapons, taken part in gang fights, smoked marijuana, and used other drugs. She describes herself as an alcoholic. Pammy also has a history of prostitution.

Findings

Slightly over half, or 57 percent, of the runaways reported having been arrested, with 43 percent having spent time in jail or in juvenile hall. As the cases of Marie, Dave, and Pammy illustrate, the extent of involvement in delinquent activities appears related to the length of time that runaways spend on their own away from their families. We found that the longer the runaways had been away from home, the more likely they were to report arrest and having had trouble with the law.

Our assessment of whether familial physical abuse was related to involvement in delinquent activities indicated no significant differences for both male and female runaways. Regardless of whether or not the runaway left because of physical abuse, a certain amount of delinquent activity was found.

We also assessed whether the runaways' experiencing sexual abuse was related to involvement in delinquent activities; again we found no significant differences on our indicators. However, when we controlled the relationship between sexual abuse and indicators of delinquent activities for gender, we did find a relationship between delinquency and sexual abuse for the female runaways in our study.

Sexual Abuse and Delinquency: Gender Differences

Gender differences in runaway behaviors as they relate to sexual victimization is underreported in the literature. We examined the impact of sexual victimization in the runaway population by studying its relationship to indicators of delinquent activities within each gender category.

Sexual abuse was considered affirmed if the adolescent reported (1) having had sex against his/her will, (2) having been sexually molested, or (3) having been forced to view the sex act, as in pornographic films. Indicators of delinquent activities included whether the runaway had (1) experienced trouble with the law that meant staying in jail or juvenile hall, (2) participated in physical violence, and (3) experienced arrest.

Of 55 females, 73 percent reported sexual abuse, compared with 38 percent of the 89 males. The higher rate for females can be attributed to their being more likely than males both to experience childhood sexual abuse and to encounter sexual abuse subsequent to running away.

As the results in table 4–2 show, our assessment of the relationship between sexual abuse and delinquent activities provides evidence that sexually abused females were more likely to engage in this behavior than their nonabused counterparts. They were significantly more likely than nonsexually abused females to report having had trouble with the law, to have participated in acts of physical violence, and to have experienced arrest. (The compounding factor of two of the indicators, trouble with the law and arrest experience, having involved the runaway activity itself was eliminated by

Table 4–2
Delinquent Activities of Abused and Nonabused Male and Female Runaways

	Males		Females	
	%	(n)	%	(n)
Had trouble with the law that meant staying in jail or in juvenile hall				
Sexually abused	55	(33)	44	(39)*
Not sexually abused	48	(54)	0	(15)
Participated in acts of physical violence				
Sexually abused	65	(34)	55	(40)*
Not sexually abused	62	(55)	13	(15)
Experienced arrest				
Sexually abused	71	(34)	43	(40)*
Not sexually abused	76	(54)	0	(15)

*p < .01

the fact that running away from home is not a status offense in Toronto. There were no statistically significant differences noted in delinquent activities for male runaways who had been sexually abused vs. male runaways who had not been sexually abused.

A strong and consistent finding from our study was that sexually abused female runaways were more likely than nonabused female runaways to engage in delinquent activities. This suggests that running away in itself does not necessarily result in deviate behaviors for female runaways.[39] Rather, it is the element of sexual abuse that is highly associated with this behavior.

There appears to be agreement in recent literature that females generally are less likely than males to be involved in delinquent behaviors of almost every variety.[40-46] Although the female delinquency rate has increased over the past few decades, the rise is mainly due to increases in arrests in the categories of petty larceny, liquor violations, and marijuana use.[47-51] Indeed, as Steffensmeir and Steffensmeir point out, female adolescents rarely deviate, but when they do, they commit petty thefts or tend to act out sexually (i.e., they more frequently violate female sex role expectations than criminal statutes).[52] These minor acts of deviance are viewed as challenges to the authority of the family and other social institutions.[53,54]

Given traditional sex differences in the nature of delinquent acts, our findings suggest that sexually abused females will be likely to engage in such delinquent activities as substance abuse, petty theft, and prostitution. The finding that sexually abused females are more likely than their nonabused counterparts to participate in acts of physical violence indicates that some female victims may cross over into the traditionally male realm of criminal activities.

Our explanation of why sexual abuse influences delinquent behavior for females but not for males is based on differences in sex role socialization that produce different reactions to familial sexual abuse. Running away as a reaction to sexual abuse is more closely associated in the literature with females.[55-57] However, while female runaways are more often victims of familial sexual abuse,[58] male victims are more likely to make attempts to run away from abusive situations.[59,60]

This gender difference in reaction to sexual abuse may result from several factors: (1) the majority of females still experience traditional patterns of socialization that relegate them to protected, dependent positions within the family structure; (2) in traditional female childhood socialization, females are denied many socially acceptable mechanisms for displaying aggressive behaviors; and (3) for female adolescents, there are prevalent social sanctions against leaving home. Thus, the experiencing of familial sexual abuse for females is likely to be more prolonged than that for males. Further, given the particular vulnerability of females trying to survive in unprotected environments, female runaways are more likely than male runaways to have the experience of sexual abuse reinforced after leaving home.

It is suggested in the literature that prolonged sexual abuse may be related to the development of aggressive personality characteristics.[61] The fact that female victims of sexual abuse may be reluctant to run away from an abusive home situation, thus prolonging this experience, and that once they do run away they are at high risk for repeated abuse may account for the aggressive behaviors indicated by participation in delinquent activities.

Both abused and nonabused male runaways engage in high levels of delinquent activities, suggesting that this is more a strategy for survival on the streets than a reaction to experiencing sexual abuse. However, sexually abused male runaways evidenced a different set of symptoms, which suggests a more insidious reaction.

Reactions of Males to Sexual Abuse

The sexual abuse of males has received limited attention in the literature and has been addressed primarily through isolated case histories,[62-69] survey studies,[70-74] and specific notices in clinical populations. Previously unreported and untreated sexual abuse is frequently mentioned in the case histories of hospitalized psychiatric populations,[75-77] rapists,[78] multiple personalities,[79] juvenile offenders,[80-86] adolescent runaways,[87] self-mutilation victims,[88-91] female prostitutes,[92-94] male prostitutes,[95] hospital emergency room patients,[96,97] and suicidal adolescents.[98]

David Finkelhor has reviewed the survey data from nonclinical populations and has concluded that, based on current information, between 2.5 percent and 8.7 percent of the general population of males have been sexually victimized as children.[99] Nowhere near this number of males has either self-reported or been brought for treatment, as Finkelhor's study of reported populations indicates. However, the high numbers indicated by this literature survey combined with the serious implications of sexual abuse have made the study of both long-term and short-term effects of sexual abuse on males an issue of prime concern. Furthermore, the connection between running away and sexual abuse in a population of males has seldom been examined.

The 34 males in our study who reported sexual abuse were compared on the basis of available demographic data to 55 males who did not report sexual abuse. There were no significant differences between those males who reported sexual abuse and those who did not on the demographic variables age, race, number of times run away, age when first left home, and time away from home.

The eight subscales of the Piers-Harris self-concept scale were administered. Sexually abused males registered lower scores but did not differ from nonabused runaways with any degree of significance on six of the eight subscales (behavioral self-esteem, intellectual and school status, physical appearance and attributes, anxiety, self-esteem, and popularity). They did score significantly lower on the subscale for happiness and satisfaction than did their nonsexually abused counterparts ($t = 1.94$; $p < .06$). This subscale, according to Piers, taps general satisfaction with life and is associated with general dissatisfaction, feelings of negative self-worth, and a longing for things to be different.[100]

Tests developed by the Langley Porter Institute to measure subjective stress, presumptive stress, and coping behaviors were administered. On the scale differentiating the type of response elicited by the impact of the traumatic event (running away from home), sexually abused males differed significantly in reporting avoidant feelings ($t = 3.08$; $p < .01$). Avoidant feelings include trying to forget about the event, blocking out feelings concerning the event, and avoiding people who reminded the runaway about the event.[101]

There were few differences in the responses of sexually abused and nonsexually abused male runaways in response to a life-events inventory. However, there were two life events for which significant differences were noted: sexually abused males more often reported the death of a father (24% vs. 9%; $p < .06$) and were offered money to have sex with an adult (58% vs. 33%; $p < .02$).

The adolescent behavior checklist asked respondents to rank a range of behaviors. Sexually abused male runaways differed significantly from nonsexually abused male runaways in their reports about their relationships with other people and their sexual feelings. Sexually abused males had more difficulty with their sexual feelings (21% vs. 11%) and their relationships with people of the same sex (48% vs. 36%) and the opposite sex (36% vs. 24%), had a significant tendency to fear adult men (35% vs. 13%), had greater trouble with school officials and employers (85% vs. 70%), and withdrew from their friends more often (55% vs. 44%) than did their nonabused counterparts.

Sexually abused male runaways more frequently reported a wider range of physical and emotional symptomatology than did nonsexually abused male runaways. These symptoms included headaches (47% vs. 29%), stomachaches (41% vs. 25%), suicidal feelings (53% vs. 34%), and tension (82% vs. 61%).

The severity of certain indicators of family distress were found to be increased in families of sexually abused males. Sexually abused males differed from nonsexually abused males in their reports of family financial problems (59% vs. 42%), arrest and/or court appearances (47% vs. 24%), serious arguments (97% vs. 85%), divorce (71% vs. 70%), and remarriage (59% vs. 38%).

The population of male runaways studied had dramatically higher rates of sexual abuse than previously studied random populations (38.2% vs. 2.5–8.7%). This clearly designates male runaways as a vulnerable population with a high risk of previous sexual abuse.

Sexually abused male runaways were more likely to be offered money to have sex with an adult, which exposes them to repeated sexual exploitation through prostitution. Repeated sexual exploitation as a sequela of child sexual abuse has been reported in cases of males with histories of sexual abuse.[102,103]

In summary, our findings on male runaways confirmed that sexually abused and nonsexually abused male runaways shared characteristics noted in the literature as common to runaways: problem families; high rates of delinquency; feelings of depression, tension, and being down on themselves; and high rates of physical abuse. Although there were no demographic differences between male runaways who had reported sexual abuse and male runaways who did not make that report, there were marked differences between the two groups in their reactions to the experience of running away.

Sexually abused male runaways scored significantly lower on the Piers-Harris measure of happiness and satisfaction, a finding consistent with previously reported symptoms.[104] As measured by the Langley Porter scales, reactions to the runaway event showed highly avoidant patterns, clearly associated with the silent reactions to sexual abuse described by Burgess and Holmstrom.[105]

Most striking was the youths' difficulty with all types of interpersonal relationships, a difficulty that includes withdrawal from relationships and fear of adult men. This latter finding, also reported by Rogers and Terry,[106] has several possible explanations: (1) the victim's fear of the perpetrator generalizes to other adult men, (2) the victim's fear of identifying with the perpetrator generalizes to fear of all adult men, and (3) the sexual exploitation by another male may elicit homophobic reactions.[107] Lack of information about the gender of the abusers in our study limits our interpretation of this finding.

Sexually abused male runaways were less likely than their nonabused counterparts to feel that the events leading to their running away were something they could have controlled and less likely to believe that they could have changed those events. Still, they were more likely to believe that they were the ones to blame for those events.[108] This association between extended abuse and perceptions of not being in control also has been noted in the literature.[109–111]

From our data, we can conclude that sexually abused male runaways find themselves in the difficult position of understanding the events that led to their running away as somewhat out of their control but as events for which they nevertheless feel responsible. We suggest that young adolescent males, who are socialized to have power and be in control, particularly in sexual situations, have no socially sanctioned avenue for integrating and recovering from an experience of sexual victimization.[112]

The varied symptoms evidenced by the sexually abused male runaways are consistent with the symptoms associated with unresolved and untreated sexual abuse. More specifically, they appear consistent with the so-called silent reaction to sexual abuse, a reaction that occurs when sexual victimization has not been reported or treated. This diagnosis is characterized by the following symptom pattern:

1. The patient shows signs of increasing anxiety as the interview progresses, such as long periods of silence, blocking of associations, minor stuttering, and physical distress.
2. The patient reports sudden, marked irritability, actual avoidance of relationships with men, or marked changes in sexual behavior.
3. The patient has a history of sudden onsets of phobic reactions and a fear of being alone, going outside, or being alone inside.
4. The patient exhibits a persistent loss of self-confidence and self-esteem, an attitude of self-blame, paranoid feelings, or nightmares and/or dreams of violence.[113]

A Final Word

Runaways evidence many varied symptoms that traditionally have been seen as the source of the conflict with home that instigated the running behavior. We have discovered that there is some order to these symptoms. In fact, these symptoms are organized around specific victimizing events in the youths' lives and are in some sense differentiated by event and gender. Victims of familial abuse evidence symptoms consistent with post-traumatic stress disorder. Sexually abused females are apt to respond to abuse with the development of aggressive personality characteristics that manifest themselves in delinquent behavior. By contrast, sexually abused males are apt to respond to the abuse with an avoidant stance similar to that found in silent and unreported cases of sexual abuse.

5
Drawings by Runaway Youths

The use of drawings as a method for developing a therapeutic alliance has been deemed useful in clinical intervention with traumatized children. The drawings have aided in reducing tension and trauma during both self-disclosure and the subsequent treatment phase.[1-4]

In our study, which assessed the human figure drawings of 128 runaway adolescents, we found that the drawing process provided an indirect and less threatening way of developing rapport. Most notably, the drawing activity appeared to act as an anxiety-reducing agent, and functioned as a vehicle that seemed to pull together the runaways' feelings and their expressions of those feelings. As Stember has noted, expressing thoughts through art is one way to externalize a distressing event and to prepare for healing and recovery.[5]

Our study examined the drawing process to determine its utility as an expressive vehicle for disclosure of psychological distress. We attempted to identify characteristics of the adolescents' drawings that would assist clinicians in the assessment of personality and behavioral responses of physically and sexually abused youth when viewed within the context of the drawing gestalt, the adolescent's gender, age, intelligence, neurological status, and family background.

Each adolescent in our study was asked to draw a picture of a whole person on a piece of white paper. Subjects were allowed to choose pencil, pen, or crayons as drawing implements. The runaways' comments were recorded prior to, during, and after completion of the human figure drawing. The drawings were independently evaluated by three art therapists. The abuse histories as well as comments made by the adolescents while drawing were not made available to these therapists during the rating procedure.

Initial resistance by the runaways to the drawing exercise was minimal and consisted of such responses as "I can't draw" and "I haven't drawn in years." This was usually followed by the comment, "but I'll try." Of the 149 adolescent runaways in our study, 128 consented to attempt the drawing exercise.

This chapter was contributed by Judith Wood Howe, M.S., A.T.R.

The drawings completed by the runaways were examined for such assessment indicators as graphic categories of gender, figure completion, line quality, and use of color. These indicators were used to compare the drawings of youths with differing personal histories of abuse (no abuse, physical abuse only, both physical and sexual abuse, and sexual abuse only).

The personal abuse histories of the youths also were compared by graphic indicators of sexual anxiety. Each drawing was coded for graphic evidence of sexual concern, curiosity, and/or anxiety.

Additionally, each drawing was assigned a behavioral category, defined as a precursor to a diagnostic category. Because of the exploratory nature of this assessment, we believed it premature to determine whether certain indicators represented either a traditional diagnostic category or a response to a specific event or series of events. Thus, our criteria for determination of behavioral categories were developed after a careful assessment of the literature for graphic descriptions that represented a consensus of agreement between two or more sources. Eleven behavioral categories, plus an open-ended category, were used. Only drawings that were placed in the same behavioral category by at least two of the three art therapists were assigned to that category. Ninety-five percent of the runaways were assigned behavioral categories in this manner.

The behavioral categories most often assessed through the drawings were (1) anxious avoidant ($n = 39$), (2) avoidant ($n = 26$), and (3) anxious ($n = 12$) (see table 5–1). We next examined the relationship between sexual abuse and behavioral category by comparing drawings by youths reporting sexual abuse ($n = 63$) with those not reporting sexual abuse ($n = 61$). The results indicate minimal differences between the groups.

To achieve a larger cell size for analysis, we collapsed the eleven behavioral categories. There was sufficient overlapping of certain graphic indicators within the categories to allow some categories to be combined, and two categories were omitted because they did not represent behavioral categories. The results of the regrouping are the following four classifications: (1) anxious avoidant, (2) anxious aggressive, (3) avoidant, and (4) disorganized. Using these four categories to compare sexually abused youths with nonsexually abused youths, we found a statistically significant difference between the two groups ($\bar{X} = 8.454, df = 3, p < .05$) (see table 5–2).

Discussion

The large number of runaways who chose to respond to the draw-a-person task (86%) and the relative ease with which the task appeared to elicit spontaneous associations from the youths about current stresses, life on the street, and past experiences with home and family, all of which may have contrib-

Table 5-1
Behavioral Categories in Runaways' Drawings

Behavioral Category	n	Distribution (%)
Anxious avoidant	39	31
Avoidant	26	21
Anxious	12	10
Avoidant aggressive	10	8
Anxious aggressive	9	7
Organicity	9	7
Disorganized	5	4
Mentally deficient	2	2
Aggressive	2	2
Disorganized aggressive	2	2
Adjusted for age	1	1
Other	1	1
No consensus	6	5

Table 5-2
Sexual Abuse and Behavioral Categories in Runaways' Drawings*
(percent)

Behavioral Category	Sexual Abuse (n = 53)	No Sexual Abuse (n = 50)
Anxious avoidant	51	38
Anxious aggressive	19	8
Avoidant	28	42
Disorganized	2	12

*$\bar{X} = 8.454$; $df = 3$; $p < .05$.

uted to the decision to run away, support the contention that the drawing process represents a nonthreatening, tension-reducing vehicle for communication that may be especially useful with the adolescent runaway population. The indirect, task-oriented structure of the drawing experience appears to defuse the anxiety generated by direct, one-on-one contact with an adult, anxiety that would likely be particularly high in troubled youths who come from severely disturbed family environments.

Behavioral Categories

By providing new data, our study responds to critical reports that question the validity of the draw-a-person task as a measure of psychological functioning in children.[6-9] It attempts to begin to define the task's measurable limits by demonstrating a distinction between the diagnostic behavioral categories for sexually abused runaways and those categories for nonsexually abused youths. (However, the limitations of our study population should be considered.)

Identification of the anxious avoidant behavioral category corresponds to the finding of Burgess and colleagues of four patterns of response to traumatic sexual abuse in childhood. This 1984 study suggests that anxiety about a traumatic event may not be integrated into the life experiences of the child victim and may remain consciously or unconsciously sealed off, thereby fostering a pattern of avoidance in the child.[10] Our finding of the anxious avoidant category directs attention to the importance of line quality in conjunction with other graphic indicators. It is notable that the sexually abused youths' drawings frequently showed evidence of graphic avoidant techniques (i.e., omissions of body parts) as well as of generalized passivity/anxiety in line quality, rendering each image somewhat compromised with regard to its expression of self-assertion. Future refinement of the graphic behavioral typology (see table 5–3) seems warranted and should take into consideration not only the demographic aspects of the subjects but also aspects of the abuse (age of onset, duration, relationship to the perpetrator, etc.). The development of the typology is a first attempt to organize graphic characteristics into a behavioral framework based on prior interpretations taken from the existing literature. Future refinement of these categories may be required and expected.

Table 5–3
Graphic Behavioral Typology for Runaways' Drawings

Integrated
   Firm, free-flowing lines
   Full figure
   Flexible use of color
   Symmetry of figure
   Age and cultural congruence of detail

Anxious
   Broken, sketchy line quality
   Prominent shading
   Tiny figures
   Emphasis on facial and body features
   Hair emphasis
   Short arms
   Legs pressed together
   Crossed legs
   Ambiguity in sexual identity
   Obsessional clothing detail (designs, stripes)
   Pencil slashes
   Slanting figure

Avoidant
  Firm line quality for body part drawn, with omission of body parts
  Profile position
  Stick figure
  Animals, monsters, or grotesque figures drawn instead of human figure
  Hiding of body parts (glasses, hands in pockets, covered eyes)
  Arms clinging to side of body

Anxious avoidant
  Broken, sketchy line quality with omission of such body parts as mouth, legs, neck, feet, arms, nose, half of face, body, pupils

Aggressive
  Bold lines, outlining
  Teeth emphasis
  Long arms
  Big hands
  Outstretched fingers
  Large feet
  Pointed feet
  Hostile effect

Anxious aggressive
  Bold, broken line quality in combination with large, exaggerated body parts or additional objects in drawing

Disorganized
  Inconsistent line quality
  Repetition of lines and objects
  Peculiar, bizarre, fantastic figure
  Eyes placed at sides of head
  Evidence of depersonalization, mechanical or lifeless figure, lacking in kinesthetic implications
  Figure details are incongruent (e.g., figure appears regressed)

Organicity
  (One or several of the following:)
  Heavy-pressed line quality
  Gross immaturity of drawing
  Parts of figure not integrated
  Emptiness of facial expression
  Lack of details
  Flattened heads
  Displacement of figure extremeties
  Petal-like or scribbled fingers and toes

Mentally deficient
  Bold, continuous line character
  Simple or primitive form concepts, but good motor coordination
  Minimal spatial gestalt characteristics
  Emotional exaggeration, omission, or distortion of form

The veritable explosion of newly disclosed cases of sexual abuse has led to the need for a noninvasive, objective assessment procedure that is both reliable and sensitive to a youngster's response to abuse. Criticism of the use of projective tests in general and of drawings in particular has handicapped progress in this assessment area. Our findings suggest that assessment through drawings be reexamined as the area of child sexual abuse becomes more accessible to study.

Case Examples

Though factors other than—or in addition to—abuse must be considered in each drawing, the following are examples of drawings completed by the runaways in our study, organized by category of abuse. As one examines the drawings, first those of runaways with no reported history of abuse, then those of runaways with physical abuse, followed by the category of combined physical and sexual abuse, and finally sexual abuse only, it becomes increasingly apparent how deeply affected is the self-image of the sexually abused child.

No Abuse

Annie is an eighteen-year-old, white female who is a high-school graduate. She has run away from home twice, the first time at age sixteen, and had been away from home for five months at the time of our interview. She reports no

Drawing 1

history of physical abuse, but speaks of verbal abuse and an unhappy life at home. The figure that she drew (see drawing 1) is well integrated with firm, free-flowing lines; it is a symmetrical, full-figure drawing with age-appropriate detail. The drawing includes associations characteristic of the interests of today's youth culture: "I invented these eyes a long time before *Garfield*."

Barry is an eighteen-year-old, white male who has a ninth-grade education. He ran away from home at age fifteen and had been away from home for three years at the time of interview. He reports no history of abuse and states that he left home to live with his girlfriend. His drawing is well integrated with firm, free-flowing lines and is a symmetrical, full-figure image with flexible use of color (see drawing 2). There is a touch of humor; the figure lifts his thumb in a gesture the runaway states is "like the Fonz." It is interesting that the figure has long hair and some evidence of breast development and that the left hand appears to cover the genitals. This may suggest some sexual identity confusion. In assessing this drawing, however, one should consider the cultural contribution to the image of long hair as well as the moderate degree of anxiety associated with sexuality appropriate to the youth's phase of adolescent development.

Among the drawings placed in the no abuse category, certain imagery was puzzling because of a lack of image integrity or a deterioration in the completeness of the human figure. Drawing 3 was done by Charles, an eighteen-year-old, white male who had run away twice, the first time at age fourteen. The drawing is a full face, yet the body image appears to fragment and is left unfinished. Perhaps his history explains the drawing. The youth's mother died when he was thirteen years old, and his father was imprisoned a year later. The boy was placed in a group home and ran away a few months later.

In some cases, the experience of a significant loss of a parental figure, (either through divorce, death, or imprisonment) and thus the partial or total collapse of an already-stressed support system appeared to wield a powerful blow to the adolescent's often poorly developed capacity to cope with his or her environment. The human figure drawings functioned as a mirror reflecting the vulnerability of the adolescent's self-structure.

Drawing 4 was completed by an eighteen-year-old male with a ninth-grade education. Tom had run away twice, the first time at twelve years of age. His drawing of the "grim reaper" is puzzling, as the youth reports no history of abuse. The youth's responses to self-report survey instruments include references to flashbacks, suicidal thoughts, feelings of going crazy and being different, and physical and verbal fights with peers. Perhaps his history also explains the drawing, and includes divorced parents, an imprisoned father, and his own six-year confinement to a correctional facility. In addition, we question whether he and perhaps other runaways may have withheld or repressed information about their abuse history.

Drawing 2

Drawing 3

Physical Abuse Only

Evidence of aggression was apparent in many drawings by youths who reported physical abuse. The remarkable human figure in drawing 5 was completed by John, an eighteen-year-old, white male who had run away five times. The image is notable for its sharp edges and, perhaps, the suggestion of a fusion of sexuality with aggression as evidenced by the acute delineation of feet, hands, tongue, and penis. John's responses on the survey instrument attest to difficulties in school and with the police, along with multiple references to depressive feelings.

Certain drawings appeared to convey a conflict between assertiveness and aggression, and we continued to view the profound impact the adolescents experienced at the loss of a significant parent. Drawing 6 was completed by Ronnie, an eighteen-year-old, physically abused, white male who had run away seventeen times, the first time at age thirteen. Depression, flashbacks, and thoughts of suicide characterize his self-report survey responses. The image he drew is well integrated, with bold lines especially in the lower half of the body. The figure conveys a sense of power and virility, a man with significant musculature. Yet the barbells are placed in a protective

Drawing 4

Drawing 5

Drawing 6

position covering the genitals. The combination of the runaway's depression and thoughts of suicide, the protective placement of the barbells, the use of the color black in the lower half of the body with the heavy outlining perhaps serving a containing or protective function, and the illustration of powerful musculature raises questions concerning a need to compensate for a deep sense of vulnerability. According to Ronnie, his reason for running away was "because my mother died. She committed suicide."

The image in drawing 7 was made by twenty-year-old George, a white male who first ran away from home at age sixteen and who has left home a total of four times. In addition to a report of physical abuse, George's depression and suicidal thoughts are apparent in his survey responses. He states that his mother left him on his own and moved to another city when he was sixteen. Aggression is apparent in the image that he drew and is indicated by the open mouth and prominent teeth. Nonseeing eyes have been widely interpreted as indications of depression, emotional immaturity, and dependency, all of which may be accurate in this case. We view the portrayal of the sightless eyes along with the omission of the body as an avoidant technique that deflects the youth's anxiety and sense of vulnerability concerning his own body and self-concept.

Drawing 7

Physical and Sexual Abuse

Drawing 8 was completed by eighteen-year-old Thomas, a white male who has been both physically and sexually abused. He has run away from home twice and had been away from home for eight months at the time of our interview. Depression characterizes his self-report survey responses. His drawing is of interest for the figure's musculature and the youth's apparent attempt to convey a powerful, aggressive countenance. However, the missing hands and the somewhat obsessional covering of the face and body with hair convey a conflictual, anxiety-ridden message of uncertainty over the expression of assertiveness or aggression.

A combination of both anxious and avoidant graphic techniques as well as anxious and aggressive graphic characteristics appeared more frequently in the drawings of youths who had been both physically and sexually abused. Anxiety was notable in line quality, particularly in broken, sketchy lines on human figures.

Drawing 9 illustrates this anxiety and shows evidence of avoidant characteristics (omission of the body, hidden eyes). The runaway initially drew the eyes, then covered them with dark glasses, and finally hid facial detail by adding facial hair and shading. One senses an approach-avoidance style of relating in this image. The figure was drawn by Stuart, a seventeen-year-old, white male with a ninth-grade education who had run away from home twice. Depression and suicidal thoughts characterize his self-report survey responses. Stuart referred to a suicide attempt in the past and to involvement with the police and juvenile court system. He states, "If a person is always being put down, the pressure keeps building up and you find some way out. A lot of people kill themselves instead of leaving home if the pressure is too great."

The figure in drawing 10 was completed by seventeen-year-old Cheryl. Cheryl first ran away at four years of age; she stayed away for eighteen hours. She reported having run away a total of *110* times, and at the time of our interview she had been away from the institution where she had been living for three months. Her history revealed physical and sexual abuse by her father for a period of ten years. Cheryl's self-report survey responses are characterized by depression, flashbacks, and suicidal thoughts. Her drawing is a partial figure of an unclothed male. The line quality conveys an impulsive quality, and includes the reworking of certain body parts, such as the nose. Cheryl reports that she was removed from probation this summer.

The use of avoidant techniques was especially evident in drawings by runaways who reported sexual abuse. The omissions of portions of the human figure may be avoidant techniques that deny the anxiety-provoking body parts.

Cathy is a twenty-year-old, white female who first ran away at age fourteen, has run away three times, and at the time of interview had been away

Drawing 8

Drawing 9

Drawing 10

Drawing 11

from home for three years. Her history reveals physical and sexual abuse, parental divorce, and constant fights with her stepfather. Her drawing (see drawing 11) is of interest for both the sketchy line quality and the omission of the body and half of the face. Although the drawing is stylistic in execution, the omissions serve to eliminate feelings of anxiety associated with a more complex rendering of the human figure.

Sarah is a twenty-year-old, white female who ran away for the first time at age eighteen. At the time of interview, she had been away from home for over one year. Sarah's self-report describes physical and sexual abuse, imprisonment of family members, difficulties with the juvenile courts, suicidal thoughts, sleep problems, and feelings of being nervous and jittery. Her human figure drawing (see drawing 12) is markedly primitive, poorly developed, and has no evidence of gender differentiation. The mouth and nose are prominent. The drawing raised questions as to perceptual difficulties in the visual motor sphere and/or the presence of serious psychological deterioration.

Drawing 12

Drawing 13

Alice is a seventeen-year-old, white female who had first run away at age eleven, reported having run away forty times, and at the time of interview had been away from home for one year. Depression and suicidal thoughts characterize her self-report responses, which include references to flashbacks, blanking out, feelings of going crazy, and feelings of unattractiveness and ugliness. Alice also had difficulties with the juvenile court system. Her drawing (see drawing 13) is notable for its animalistic, nonhuman appearance as well as the omission of the figure's body. Alice describes the figure as a "devil," and she states that she thinks of the devil as a person. The drawing's oral aggression is notable. Alice's history includes rape and physical abuse, and her drawing raises concerns over a significant personality disturbance.

A particularly poignant and expressive drawing (drawing 14) was completed by Anna, a seventeen-year-old, North American Indian girl who reported that this was her first runaway experience. She had been away from her foster home for three days. Her imagery conveys her sadness, and perhaps despair, as the figure hides her head on her knees. She states, "They [her foster parents] were like all the other parents. They just gave up on me; they didn't want me anymore."

Drawing 14

Sexual Abuse Only

In drawings by runaways who reported a history of sexual abuse only, avoidant techniques (i.e., omissions of body parts), anxiety, and evidence of conflict over expression of assertiveness were notable. The drawings also conveyed a sense of helplessness.

Jack is a seventeen-year-old, white male who has run away from home three times this year. His history includes sexual abuse. Jack's self-report responses are of interest for their limited associations and include statements suggesting withdrawal and passivity (i.e., feeling worried or tense, keeping feelings inside, feeling down on himself, and having little interaction with peers). His human figure drawing (see drawing 15) is notable for both anxious and avoidant graphic characteristics, with shading on the lower part of the body and genital area; an absence of pupils, hands, and feet; and an omission of clothes on the upper body.

Kevin is a twenty-year-old, white male who first ran away at age thirteen and has run away five times. His self-report profile is similar to Jack's; there are minimal associations as well as expressions of depression, keeping feelings inside, and difficulties in relationships with male peers. Kevin has been sexually abused. The imagery in his drawing (see drawing 16) is notable for the omission of the body, a faint line quality, a somewhat mixed message of approach avoidance (the wink serves to hide one eye), and an overall drawing gestalt of minimal self-assertion.

Lance is an eighteen-year-old, white male who ran away for the first time at age seventeen. Self-report survey responses include statements of keeping feelings inside, of not having much interaction with friends, and of feeling lonely. His history indicates he was sexually abused. Lance describes himself as suicidal in the past, closely bonded to his mother, and as having been hospitalized several times for self-inflicted injuries. The imagery in his drawing (see drawing 17) is interesting in the use of avoidant techniques (body omission and hidden eyes) and in the youth's attempt to illustrate an idealized peace activist and proponent of nonviolence, John Lennon.

Terry is a twenty-year-old, white female who ran away for the first time at age fifteen, has run away four times, and at the time of interview had been away from home for six months. Her self-report responses reflect depression, suicidal thoughts, difficulty interacting with peers, tuning out, and feeling afraid of adult men. Terry has been sexually abused, and she feared she was pregnant at the time of interview. The human figure she drew (see drawing 18) is notably primitive and lacking in gender differentiation other than an apparent skirt on the figure. The figure's pupils are omitted. The drawing conveys a sense of helplessness, and aggression appears muted.

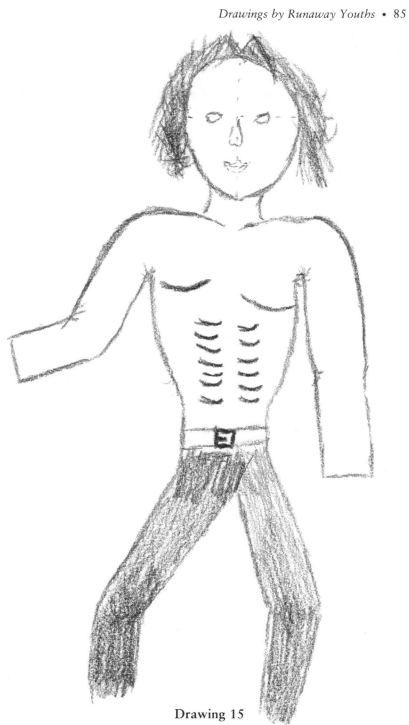

Drawing 15

Drawing 16

Drawing 17

Drawing 18

6
Pathways and Cycles of Runaways: Youths and Their Beliefs about Running Away

On their own, unable to provide for themselves for an extended period of time, without concrete or specific plans for their futures, and with no solid sense of identity, runaways become part of that ambiguous mass of the socially lost—our missing children, our homeless. Yet despite the reasons for their venturing prematurely from their homes, most runaways return. Many return and run away again and again. This chronic running away pattern is particularly true for those youths who run away from abusive home environments—for those who run for their lives.

Running away has been previously described as a response to abuse.[1] On the surface, this statement seems simple. Yet its complexity resides in the fact that runaways who are abused and run away frequently return home, only to run away again. In attempting to describe patterns of running and to isolate the factors that support the running phenomenon, we not only have to ask why youths run away from home, but also the equally compelling question, Why do they return home? As a result of study findings concerning these two questions, this chapter presents a model that considers repetitious runaway behavior and attachment to an abusive environment. The means of traumatic event processing and the pathways and cycles for running away are discussed. We suggest that the cognitive style of runaways, which emerges out of the context of family and social life, acts as a mediating factor in the cyclic running phenomenon.

An important consideration guiding our research on the runaway population concerns understanding the repetitive behavior that resulted in a negative outcome. One approach to understanding repetitive behavior is that behavior repeats itself because the individual does not perceive alternatives or feel in control. An individual does feel in control when one or more of the following is present: (1) the person knows of specific actions or has a repertoire of actions to take; (2) the person has some sense of the predictability of events, of his or her own efforts, or of the actions of others; and (3) the individual has some basic understanding of what is happening now and what can be expected to happen in the future. Because runaways are not known for their planning skills but instead manifest an orientation to the present, it seems reasonable that a preliminary investigation of their causal beliefs about why they ran away and their presuppositions regarding control, predictability, and accountability might help define the cognitive mediating parameters of their actions.

Earlier investigations into the roles of beliefs and behavior and into possible methods of tapping this interactive domain were sponsored by Rotter and focused on the concept of locus of control. This concept suggests that each time a person's behavior is followed by an expected outcome, there is an increase in the individual's expectation that the behavior and outcome are related. To the extent that a person's behavior is not followed by an expected outcome, there is a lack of association and a decreased expectation that one's efforts make a difference. To those individuals who have their positive expectations reinforced, the link between behavior and outcome creates a sense of internal control. Those persons who do not have their positive efforts reinforced will have a diminished sense that their efforts count. Instead, they will attribute the outcome of events to external factors, such as luck or other outside reasons.[2]

Over the past years, application of this model through Rotter's internal-external scale has produced studies reporting that expectancies influence competencies and preference feelings, shifts in levels of aspiration, and risk taking. Expectancies have also been shown to mediate perceptual, cognitive, and motivational processes.[3-8] However, other researchers reviewing the locus of control studies suggest that the internal-external scale is not predictive of dependent variables under investigation.[9] (These variables include such concepts as self-esteem, successful learning of a task, health practices, and health beliefs.)

Lowery and colleagues have reviewed the limitations of the Rotter scale and underscore the warnings advanced by Rotter.[10-12] Behaviors, expectancies, reinforcements, and situations are major variables in Rotter's model of personal perception. Behavior alone cannot be linked to whether a person is internal or external in perception of control. Response patterns (overt behaviors) are in part a function of the ambiguity and novelty of a situation as well as of its familiarity. Familiar situations can be expected to elicit more specific responses, while ambiguous and novel situations can generate more global or generalized behaviors.

The value attributed to reinforcements may be more important to behavior than an individual's locus of control orientation. For example, a mother may submit to abuse from her husband to protect her child. This example also demonstrates that a mother's perception of alternatives may be more operant in selecting a behavioral response than her perception of personal control being within her power or within the power of others.

Weiner and Russell, exploring attributions (e.g., ascribed beliefs regarding life events), paid particular attention to causal beliefs and three dimensions of these beliefs. The dimensions are: (1) whether a cause is unstable or stable, (2) whether a cause is controllable or uncontrollable, and (3) whether a cause is internal or external to the individual.[13,14] However, attempts by Weiner and Russell to create instruments to measure and capture the complexity of Rotter's original model have not resulted in measures that can predict behavior from beliefs.

Despite the lack of predictive measures, retrospective exploration of an individual's presuppositions regarding his or her causal beliefs can be useful for descriptive purposes. This is what we have done.

The conceptual basis of our research and the organization of the findings in this chapter are predicated on two important models: (1) traumatic event processing and its impact on the biopsychosocial makeup of the individual, and (2) a descriptive paradigm of the pathways and cycles of running away. Linking those two models are the runaways' beliefs concerning their reasons for running and their presuppositions regarding the control, predictability, and accountability of themselves and others regarding their reasons for running away. We believe that these models help explain the repetition of the runaway behavior and the unfortunate outcome for many of these youths.

Traumatic Event Processing

Our investigation of runaways revealed a history of physical, sexual, and verbal trauma emitting from the family, the streets, and the various institutions to which the youths ran. In prior studies of children sexually abused both within the family and in sex rings, a model was developed to account for the children's methods for coping with the traumatic event itself and for the subsequent manifestations of adjustment patterns.[15] The five components of this traumatic event processing model are: (1) preabuse factors, (2) the traumatic event(s), (3) nondisclosure, (4) disclosure, and (5) outcome behaviors (see figure 6–1). The arrows in the figure indicate the directional flow between 1 and 5; the bidirectional arrow between 3 and 4 indicates the outcome behaviors with and without disclosure.

Preabuse factors include age of the victim, personality development, social/cultural dimensions, family structure, and prior trauma. Dimensions of the *traumatic event,* which imprints the victim with the individual meaning of the event, include identity of the offender, entrapment, access to the victim, control of the victim, number of occurrences, sexual activities, and methods of maintaining secrecy about the abuse. *Nondisclosure,* referring to the time during which no one knew about the event, includes dissociation, encapsulation of the trauma, splitting, ego fragmentation, drive disharmony,

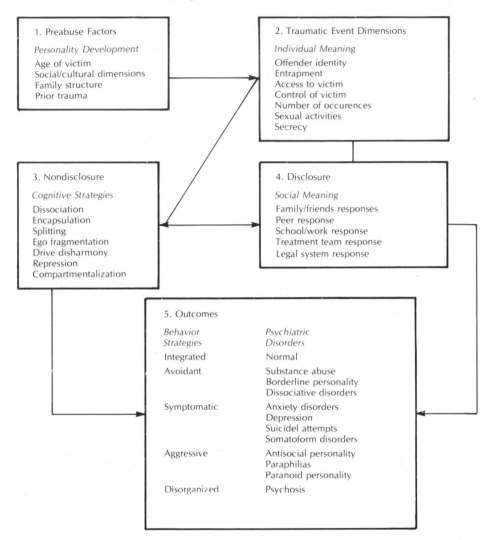

Figure 6–1. Traumatic Event Processing Model

repression, and compartmentalization. *Disclosure* is the time the event is made known to others and includes the social meaning of the abuse. It involves responses of family, friends, school or work associates, and peers as well as institutional responses (the treatment team and the legal system) to knowledge of the abuse.

One key aspect of this model is that trauma sets into motion (1) particular defensive and survival maneuvers of a cognitive/behavioral dimension and (2) physiological defensive operations. The more persistent and intense the abuse, the stronger the defensive patterns and operations.

This results in fragmentation of the psychological integrity of the individual. The *outcome* of the trauma can be one of five general behavior patterns: (1) integrated, (2) avoidant, (3) symptomatic, (4) aggressive, and (5) disorganized.

Integration of the event is marked by reasonable mastery of the traumatic event. The youth can recollect the event without excessive denial or distortion. In cases of abuse by an adult, the victim can recognize the wrongness of the adult's behavior. The youth's capacities for learning, caring, and participating in intimate relationships are positive.

The avoidant pattern is marked by the youth's minimization of the event, reluctance to discuss the event, and denial of the trauma. The youth, although able to reveal traumatic events in his or her life, does not associate them with his or her running behavior and the attempt to avoid psychological pain and terror. Rather, the youth may focus on running as a personal thrill. The trauma may be avoided consciously and/or unconsciously. If the youth has revealed the traumatic event, it is not always associated with present avoidant behavior such as running away. Drugs and alcohol are used to block memories and to reduce dysphoric states. There is confusion in the youth's mind about who is responsible, particularly in cases of abuse by an adult.

The symptomatic behavior pattern is associated with the persistence of disruptive psychological and physiological symptoms of hyperarousal. Any mention of the traumatic event elicits highly anxious behavior. These symptoms impair learning and self-development activities. The youth is confused about responsibility, particularly in cases of abuse by an adult, and extreme forms of self-blame may be present. Drugs and alcohol are used to reduce dysphoric states.

Aggressive patterns are those in which the youth does not deny the traumatic events. Instead, the event is minimized or flaunted. Most outstanding is the youth's exploitative aggression toward others. Accompanying this aggression is the youth's continuous justification for this behavior.

Disorganized patterns are those in which the youth's presentations either are or border on the psychotic. Recall of the traumatic event intensifies disorganized behavior. Often, these youths are labeled with an array of psychiatric diagnoses. There is rarely any linking of their symptoms to chronic post-traumatic stress disorder.

Pathways and Cycles of Running Away

From our data on the runaway population, we constructed a model that outlines belief patterns (i.e., cognitive structures of beliefs and expectations) and cycles of running. Our approach, which is basically descriptive, was taken in part because there is so little information on the evolution of belief patterns of runaways, as well as of physically, psychologically, and sexually abused children.[16] To illustrate the problem of why youths run away and why they return home again, a schematic model of the pathways, cycles, and outcomes of running is presented in figure 6–2.

The *pathways* represent the alternatives youths have for running away. In the four pathways identified in this study, the youth can run to or from (1) the family, (2) the institution, (3) the street, and (4) the shelter. The family can be the youth's family of origin (intact or separated) or a reconstituted family. The street represents the open environment that is unprotective, enticing, and exploitative. It includes subways, abandoned buildings, and

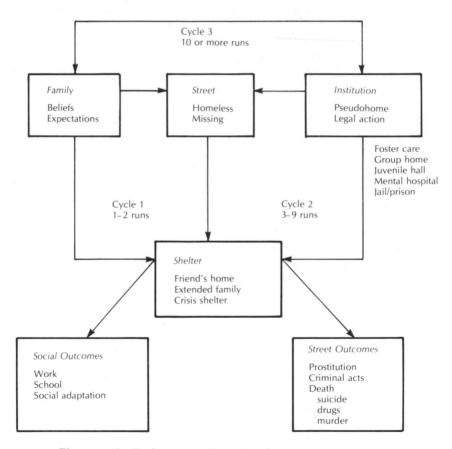

Figure 6–2. Pathways and Cycles of Runaway Youth

other temporary, unsecured living areas. Institutions are pseudohome facilities, such as foster or group homes. They may include legal or health facilities, such as juvenile hall, mental institutions, correctional facilities, or jail. The shelter is a protective, temporary arrangement that provides food, beds, and some form of companionship. It may be provided by a friend, church group, or other human service organization.

The *cycles* show how youths repeat runaway behavior or return home in a cyclical pattern through the four pathways. The primary launching base for running away for our sample was the home; 63 percent of the youths ran away from their homes to seek other shelter. Once the family is left behind, a secondary launching base can be an institution or shelter; 37 percent of the youths ran to a shelter from a foster home, group home, or detention hall. Cyclical patterns of running can be (1) family to street to shelter to family, (2) street to institution or shelter to street, or (3) institution to family or shelter to street. Variations in the cyclical pattern may be present.

There are two types of *outcomes* to running: positive and negative. Positive outcomes include social adaptation, such as work, school, or family. Some runaways are able to break out of the cycle and work sporadically (about one-third of our sample had a history of working). The negative outcome, however, is the more dominant pattern. Once on the street, the outcome can be prostitution; criminal activity; drug abuse; or death by suicide, drug overdose, or murder.

Negative Outcomes of Running Away

The results of analyzing the length of time that runaways have been away from home in relation to other variables illustrate the propensity that runaways have for negative outcomes. These outcomes include delinquent behaviors, job loss, and prostitution.

Youths away from home the longest tended to be older than those who were away from home for shorter periods of time, and those away longer were also more likely to be male. There was little relationship between time away from home and whether the youths report working. This is reasonable given the finding that youths who were away the longest were most likely to report job loss.

Youths who were away from home for over a year were more likely to report having had trouble with the law, trouble that meant spending time in jail or juvenile hall. They were also more likely to have been arrested and to have participated in physical violence than were youths away from home for a lesser period of time, although the difference in the latter case is small.

Youths who were away from home for over one year were more likely to report being offered money to have sex than were runaways who had been away for shorter periods of time. They were more likely to report sexual abuse than were those away from home between one month and one year. However, runaway youths away from home for less than one month were most likely to report being sexually abused (63%). Further exploration of this relationship indicated that there was *no* relationship between time away from home and the reporting of sexual abuse for males. For females, however, the relationship was highly significant. Of females away from home for less than one month, 86 percent reported sexual abuse, compared with 50 percent for those away from home between one month and one year. Of female runaways away from home for over one year, 91 percent reported sexual abuse. This suggests that for females in particular, sexual abuse may be a stimulus for running away and that the longer the time spent on the street, the more vulnerable the female is to this type of abuse.

The reported differences between males and females is illustrated by two treatment cases in which runaway behavior was revealed to have been important in the lives of the two abuse victims. These ancillary cases come from the private clinical practices of two of the authors.

Fred. A fifty-year-old, white male, Fred walked into a mental health clinic manifesting signs and symptoms of toxic psychosis. At first, he was guarded in relating to a male mental health worker. After a female worker took over the interview, it became clear that Fred was toxic from a dependency on the drug lithium. Several years earlier, after retiring from the military, Fred had become depressed. He saw a psychiatrist and was given lithium. Fred never returned to the psychiatrist; instead, he obtained and managed his own drug dosage. After Fred's problem with lithium was rectified, attention was focused on his depression following his retirement. Particular consideration was given to his life in the service.

Fred entered the service at age eighteen in order to escape from an alcoholic and abusive father. He had run away several times before entering the service and was always in trouble. A year after he joined the service, he was gang raped by a group of soldiers in his unit. He said that he never forgot this incident, although he never told anyone about it. He also did not tell anyone about the abuse by his father. When asked why he did not disclose any past abuse, Fred said that he tended to hold himself partly responsible for what happened. He believed that he was partly responsible because of his own interests, explorations, and fantasies about sexual matters. He then revealed a childhood history of sexual molestation perpetrated by a teenage boy. Again, Fred said that he held himself partly responsible for this early abuse because of his curiosity about sex.

Fred strongly supported the notion that boys are reluctant to admit to sexual exploitation by males because of the male attitude toward early sexual interests. Virginity is not a socially desirable state for males, and sexual exploration is tolerated if not encouraged. Thus, an exploitative sexual event can confuse a young male. Fear of recrimination, of one's own curiosity about sex, and of having one's participation revealed restricts the male from disclosing sexual abuse. This is particularly true if (as in most cases) the abuser is male.

More than young males, young females are threatened by abuse from within the family, with incest the dominating type of sexual exploitation. Threats and rejection of appeals for help affect female reporting patterns. Running away from home may become a first line of defense. The case of two sisters with histories of chronic running away behavior to escape an unbearable relationship with their stepfather contrasts with the male reporting pattern evident in the case of Fred.

Jane and Her Sister. Jane came to a feminist therapist two years after her first contact with a psychiatrist, which was prompted by her own violent attack on her female lover. The attack occurred when Jane, who was sleeping, was approached by her lover. That she would attack the woman startled Jane, and believing that she was crazy, she went to see the psychiatrist. The psychiatrist put her on drugs and left her on her own for several months. Jane did not continue with therapy.

Two years later, Jane saw a film on incest. This prompted her to contact the feminist therapist. Although Jane remembered the incest in her childhood, she never connected her recent confusion and difficulties with the earlier abuse. As Jane recalled the abuse of both herself and her sister, she also remembered earlier thoughts about her situation and how they had compelled certain life decisions.

Jane's earlier memory of being molested by her then foster father was at the age of five. She stated, "It may have been earlier. . . . I had a feeling it was something wrong . . . no word for it . . . I knew I couldn't talk about it. He would come into the bedroom at night." Jane remembered wetness on the outside of her pubic area and legs.

When Jane was in the third grade and her sister in the first, the foster parents went to court to adopt the children. Jane recalled this event: "I see myself as small and wishing someone would ask me. . . . I wish the judge would have asked." When Jane was in the fifth grade, her sister revealed that her stepfather was molesting her.

Jane remembered what she felt about revealing the abuse: "I believed that he'd go to prison. . . . It'd kill [my stepmother] and I'd break up the family. . . . We were being abused physically by our mother . . . beating us, getting us to clean in the middle of the night. . . . They had adopted a little boy, [and we saw a] real difference in [their] treatment of him . . . he was a baby. . . . Both of us agreed that we shouldn't tell. . . . We felt lucky not to be out on the street."

By the eighth grade, conflict between Jane and her stepmother had intensified, particularly over Jane's going out and having friends. "She read Ann Landers a lot." One night, in an argument with her stepmother, Jane yelled at her and screamed out what her stepfather was doing. "It got very quiet. . . . She took me down to the basement, and she took it seriously. She asked me what happened. . . . He tried to intervene but she let me talk . . . I remember it vividly. . . . I went to a friend's house or to a school event. . . . She was going to stop work. She said that she would take care of things . . . but nothing happened. . . . She did accuse her husband of being in love [with me]. . . . This stopped the incest. At the end of the year I ran away to be an aspirant at the nunnery."

"I stayed there [at the nunnery] for a year. . . . They decided that I wasn't nun material. . . . I was noisy, smoked . . . was upset . . . knew it was [because of] sex things. . . . They [my parents] were happy I was going to be a nun. [I] came back home and went to school. . . . [The] year is a blank . . . no sexual experiences . . . I wasn't at all sexual. . . . [I was] just beginning to think of dating. . . . [I] worked during that summer, then my sister came and told me that [our stepfather] was bothering her again."

"We went and told the priest about the incest. He suggested we talk to the nun who had placed us. I met with her, and she said, 'sit tight.' It [the incest] again happened to my sister. I wrote a letter to the priest . . . put the whole story in my letter. . . . My sister panicked when the letter came back. . . . I was so scared of what might happen."

"I called the priest, [and] he had me talk to a lawyer who said, 'Are you sure you aren't pregnant by a boy?' The priest agreed to talk to me. . . . I was motivated out of fear of my stepfather [and] went to the police station. [The] police referred me to the district attorney, who asked me to take a lie detector test. . . . I said yes, [and] he said he believed me."

"[My stepfather] admitted it and [they] said he was a sick man. . . . My sister and I left. . . . We were put in a cell, [which was] better than with [my stepparents]. We were then sent to a Catholic home . . . no mail [or] phone calls. . . . [I] went to court [and] testified. . . . He pleaded guilty, but they asked if I'd drop the charges. . . . I didn't know what even happened."

Jane and her sister were sent to a Catholic home, then the girls were separated. Jane ran away from the home, and when she was returned, she was placed in a foster home. She ran away from this home and was returned to the Catholic home.

Jane graduated from high school and received a college scholarship. She started college to study to be a teacher. She said that her problems began while in college. She was involved in drugs and alcohol, partying and dating. She dropped out of school, and at nineteen years of age she married a "good

Catholic boy. He appealed to me by looks and stability. . . . I left after six months. [There was] trouble with sex, [and we] even went to a doctor. . . . The marriage wasn't consummated for two months . . . I was very tight."

Jane worked and dated but did not have sex with her dates. At twenty-two she returned to college. She worked as a waitress during this time. She met a thirty-six-year-old man, whom she thought charming, and moved in with him. She determined that he was a "creep"; he claimed to be a pilot but was living on a policeman's pension and having affairs. Jane gave him money and what she termed "good sex." She stayed with him until she finished her undergraduate degree, but did stop having sex with him. Eventually, she left him and became involved with her boss, a married man.

Jane moved and became interested in mental health work. With this change, she became involved in a relationship with a woman. She now defined herself as a lesbian. Although feeling that she "got more from relationships with women," her interest in sex diminished, and she turned more to her work. Jane's use of alcohol increased, and she entered her first therapy after her violent attack on her female lover.

After beginning therapy the second time, Jane brought a lawsuit against her adoptive father for his sexual abuse. During this time, she attempted to have her sister join in the lawsuit. This was difficult for her sister, who is more gravely disturbed and has been in and out of mental institutions.

The early thoughts identified by Jane in her adult life reveal how powerful these thoughts were in shaping and organizing her psychological make up. First, she identified herself as helpless, yet lucky to be in a household despite the abuse. She had a deep sense that the sexual abuse was wrong, and was convinced that she knew this before the age of five, before she had words for what had happened. She assumed responsibility for holding the family together by keeping the secret, but longingly wished and believed that she could only reveal the secret if someone asked her, such as the judge. An important comparison was made between herself and her sister and the baby brother brought into the home. He was treated differently; he was treated better. This enforced Jane's deep belief that her femaleness was somehow at the root of her stepfather's action. At an early age, she began to hold her gender as the causal link in the exploitation and abuse by her parents.

Jane's willfulness, as well as her fears of her sexuality, broke through in adolescence. Alteration of the damage that had been done became possible when Jane told her adoptive mother about the abuse. However, response to the disclosure was most destructive. Jane's stepmother gave an initial impression of believing the girl and of doing something about the abuse, yet she put the fatal issue of responsibility on Jane when she accused the stepfather of being in love with Jane. This served to block Jane's rage and link her sense of self with the basic cause of the man's behavior.

Jane's sense of survival is demonstrated through her poignant struggle to leave home with her sister. An important issue is how the nuns, priest, law-yers, and courts all contributed to Jane's self-blame while simultaneously half-heartedly supporting both girls' efforts to leave home. The fact that the girls were coerced by the adults to drop the initial charges had a resounding effect on the personal sense of self evolving in the sisters.

Jane sought relationships with men, yet rejected the one who was most developmentally suitable and launched into a pattern of self-degrading behavior. To find peace, she unsuccessfully defined herself as a lesbian. She abstained from sex and became immersed in her work. However, depression and agitation broke through, culminating in a violent act that she now attri-butes to a basic flaw within herself—she is crazy.

The case of Jane, as well as of other people at various stages of involvement and release from sexual exploitation, substantiates the deleterious effect of sexual assault and its aftermath. In addition, the response of the victimizer toward the victim further intensifies these patterns. The victim's situation is further compromised by the response of those attending to the victim at the time of the disclosure and during the period of recovery.

The empirical knowledge related to a victim's social support system and the response of the treatment team and legal agencies becomes the basis of an integration of the cognitive/behavioral principles with the crisis model of intervention. We have found it useful to think of intervention addressing phases of the traumatic event, its disclosure, and the process of recovery. Assumptions made are that during each phase, and dependent upon the inter-action of the victim with other people at each phase, various coping mecha-nisms are used for survival. At the nonspoken level of behavior, these coping mechanisms regulate levels of body awareness and numbness. At the person-ality level, these coping mechanisms aim at defining meaning through identi-fication of the experience with a sense of self. These processes are partially revealed in the beliefs expressed by the victims and by persons within their social networks.

Cognitive Styles of Runaways: Beliefs and Expectations

Our model of pathways and cycles of runaways highlights how little stands between the runaway and the negative life outcomes of delinquent behavior, substance abuse, and prostitution. For runaways caught in the cycle, the bot-tom line is survival. Work is not a frequent accomplishment. Shelters are sought, but provide only temporary assistance. The street and shelter become mediating factors between the youth and the family or other institutions, yet neither of these environments are free of the potential for producing abuse and stress. Compounding the environment-based problems for the runaway are the youth's own beliefs about running away.

The primary premise of our model is that the runaways' internal beliefs regarding themselves and the expectations of parents or caretakers play a critical role in the cyclic phenomenon. To explore these beliefs, we presented runaways with nine general reasons for running away and asked them about the importance of each reason to their own experience of leaving home.

We asked the runaways to do three tasks regarding their beliefs about why they left home: (1) to rank their general opinion (very important, somewhat important, and not important) on nine reasons of why they believe young people in general run away from home; (2) to give their opinion on the same nine reasons as they related to why they personally ran away from home; and (3) to rank whether the reasons they ran away from home were something they or others controlled, something they could change, something that was unpredictable, and something for which they could blame themselves (a modified Russell scale).[17]

An unhappy life was ranked as a very important reason for leaving home by 54 percent of the youths ("My life was intolerable."). Fifty-one percent ranked verbal abuse as very important ("I got sick of being told off, then going back for a few days and being told that I was no good."), and 43 percent ranked physical abuse as important ("I was beaten."). Other reasons ranked as very important included the following: "Things just happen"; "I was tired of living the stereotyped way of life"; "Drugs"; "Drug-induced psychosis led me to professional help, which helped me to get out of a very stressful environment"; "alcohol"; "I needed time to clean up my act to get away from alcohol"; "God's will"; "personal thrill"; and "just do crazy things."

Other important reasons for running away were written in the blank spaces provided on the questionnaire. Several runaways gave reasons related to independence. One written response serves as a good example: "I couldn't live with the closed communication, lack of trust, arguments, pushing me too hard to do things I couldn't do or giving me many expectations. I like myself, my life-style, my attitude and outlook on life. I need inner peace to get along with people, not when someone is trying to make me into something I am not happy or relaxed with."

Verbal arguments and fighting were noted by many youths: "I had too many fights with my stepmother and my father is an alcoholic"; and several youths identified struggles over rules: "Not being allowed to live my own life and too many rules." Additional written reasons for leaving home included neglect ("I did not feel part of the family."), being told to leave ("I was unable to do things my mother expected and in turn was told to leave."), and intolerable situations ("[I] was having trouble with the kids my age around me.").

In comparing sexually abused vs. nonsexually abused runaways with the nine reasons for running away, sexually abused youths were more likely than nonsexually abused youths to list physical abuse as an important reason for leaving home (51% vs. 33%; $p < .05$). This lends support to the popular belief that sexual and physical abuse often go hand in hand.

The internal-external dimension of attribution refers to the degree to which cause is attributed to something about oneself (internal) or to other people (external). When the youths were asked their beliefs about control of events leading to running away, 76 percent believed that others were in control, 64 percent believed they could have changed things, 70 percent believed that these things were unpredictable, 54 percent blamed themselves, and 54 percent believe that they could have controlled the events (see table 6–1).

When considering these five dimensions on the modified Russell scale, sexually abused youths were less likely than their nonabused counterparts to believe they could have controlled the reasons for their running, more likely to see things as unpredictable, and less likely to believe that they could have changed things. However, the results of controlling for sex of the runaway indicated that sexually abused males were more likely to blame themselves for the events of running than were their nonabused counterparts. For females, the opposite was found; sexually abused females were much less likely to blame themselves than were their nonabused counterparts.

Table 6–1
Sexual Abuse and Beliefs about Control of Events Leading to
Running Away
(percent)

	Total	Males	Females
Things I could have controlled myself			
Sexually abused	47	55	41
Not sexually abused	62	62	62
Things were under the control of others			
Sexually abused	74	76	74
Not sexually abused	77	77	77
Things were unpredictable			
Sexually abused	77	75	79
Not sexually abused	63	62	67
Could have change things if I wanted to			
Sexually abused	57	69	47
Not sexually abused	73	76	58
No one else to blame but me			
Sexually abused	54	69*	41**
Not sexually abused	54	48	82

*$p = .06$
**$p < .05$

The belief that other people, such as family or caretakers, control events and that the events are unpredictable indicates a seriously confused perception of others, of oneself, and of what can be expected. It is this cognitive confusion that plays a major role in the thinking patterns of the runaways and that underlies their cyclical behavior. In fact, neither they nor their families can be held accountable for unpredictable events, yet they blame both the family and themselves. This confusion may stem from learned social expectations that things "should be different."

The expectation that things should be different links the youth back to the family. The runaway believes that parents should change and that he or she also should be able to change. Although a belief that things can change is essential for productive living, believing that things *should* change without sensing another person's reasonable capacities for change can only result in repeated disappointment. Change is experienced as a function of blaming. If no change occurs, there is a repetition of nonproductive behaviors and cycles of running within a context of mounting blame.

The runaway's returning home to an abusive or adverse environment is understandable behavior when one realizes that there is little basis in the youth's mind for generating alternatives. One might also speculate that time away from a painful, confusing environment is followed by a gradual forgetting, disbelieving, or questioning whether the environment at home was really as bad as remembered. This reasoning pattern may be reinforced if the runaway is confronted with adversity in the new sanctuary or shelter.

The gender differences in blame patterns (sexually abused males internalizing blame, and sexually abused females externalizing blame) suggest a differential response to sexual abuse by runaway males and females. This implies that there is a difference in type of abuse, the methods of psychologically controlling the victims, and the family dynamics, all of which support the confusing and unreasonable expectations of runaways.

While the data collected cannot establish a causal link between a child's confused structure of thinking and earlier sexual abuse, it does support clinical studies that suggest that the blame mechanism, used as a control measure by adults to sexually exploit children, impacts strongly on the child's thinking and reasoning.[18,19] By control we mean that the child has been manipulated to keep the abuse secret, to feel compelled to continue in the abusive relationship, and to refrain from acting against the abuser. The abuser selects strategies that can control a particular child. The child's sense of being exploited and abused is disqualified by the adult, and the child is led to feel responsible for the abusive events. Even though runaways may not necessarily assume responsibility for abuse, their self-destructive patterns of behavior, manifested in such actions as running away, being sexually indiscriminate, and using drugs, reveal a personal disregard.

We speculate that the majority of sexually abused female runaways were victims of intrafamilial sexual abuse, while the sexually abused runaway males were victimized outside the family. There is evidence that boys' experiences in sex rings in which they are sometimes forced to commit predatory acts on peers makes them hold themselves more accountable for participating in the sexual activity.[20] Males blaming themselves focus on issues of personal control as well as on control of their environment. They may act out their sexual exploitation; they may hide it; they may try to reduce self-blame through fantasies of sexual power and prowess. When they become the victimizer, they assume power and control and are able to reverse roles. In contrast, females' reactions to sexual entrapment in the family involve running away, even if the decision to do so is made only after prolonged abuse. Thus, they do not see themselves as responsible (they blame others), but they do see abuse as unpredictable and uncontrollable.

There is no modification of expectations or development of reasonable self-control for the runaway. Rather, the youth becomes polarized between unattainable expectations and no expectations. The adolescent becomes confused and is unable to gain perspective of self and of the social world. Sexual and physical abuse compound the confusion of an unhappy, verbally abusive, and intolerable family life. Continued victimization is reinforced by such street outcomes as prostitution, criminal activity, or even death. Only a few runaways are able to break out of the cycle and achieve a socially adaptive lifestyle.[21]

7
Helping the Runaway

Intervening in the cycle of running away presents many challenges. The fallout for the youths, their families, and society from the consequences of running away can be measured in personal tragedy and societal unrest. Drugs, alcohol, disease, and crime drain the resources of our nation. The runaways' problems are frequently complex and deep-seated, particularly among the youths who have been abused, and thus may require the services of various specialists and agencies.

The runaway needs help if the cycle of running is to be broken and the youth directed toward positive achievements. This chapter examines three aspects of providing that aid: (1) intervention considerations, (2) levels of intervention for short-term programs, and (3) long-term intervention programs.

Intervention Considerations

A runaway episode is generally not a short-term crisis, but rather the result of potentially serious problems that require clinical and social intervention. Thus, three basic tasks face the runaway and those who assume the responsibility for treating the youth: (1) assessing for possible reconciliation with the home, (2) preparing for independent living, and (3) maintaining health.

Because of the recent findings of high rates of physical and sexual abuse among runaways, persons working with these youths are faced with a complex situation. They must be alert not only to the youth's more immediate, obvious problems, but also the possibility that there may be undisclosed abuse in the youth's background. In fact, the runaway may even resist the helping efforts of concerned individuals because of untreated past abuse. Helping professionals need to appreciate the clinical differences between abused and nonabused runaways in order to develop an effective treatment plan and to overcome the runaway's resistance to participating in the planning.

The family difficulties that cause a child to leave home most often are not simple communication problems or parent-teenager disagreements. Instead, they represent serious family distress, particularly in cases of physical and sexual abuse in the home. Thus, the simplistic response of returning runaways to such families places the youths at additional risk of abuse and of subsequent runaway episodes. Helping professionals must assess thoroughly the family's ability and motivation to address problems, to accept the youth back into the family, or to help the youth to live under alternative arrangements. These are complex issues that require long-term therapeutic attention.

The very issues that make it difficult for a youth to remain within his or her family also make it difficult for the runaway to respond to outside help. First, these youths come from families that have lacked organization and structure in family intactness and that have not encouraged the youths to achieve independence. These same families have maintained rigid rules and procedures. Thus, it is very likely that the youths will have difficulty in adapting to the structured surroundings of youth shelters and group homes and will be unprepared to take part in their own treatment plan. They will associate this new experience of planned treatment and structured living with the inconsistent, rigid rules of the families they left behind. Consequently, they may displace the anger and aggression they feel toward family members and direct these feelings toward crisis intervenors.

Second, the runaways often come from families lacking in the ability to express concern and support. As a result, the runaway may appear manipulative, secretive, and untrusting. The youth will be unlikely to accept or understand the care and concern offered by the helping professional. This concern is not only distrusted, but it contrasts with the inadequacies of the youth's family, thus forcing the youth to reassess the painful aspects of the home environment.

Third, many families have not encouraged the runaways to develop skills that would allow them to succeed on their own. Consequently, these youths may not be ready to live on their own as an alternative to rejoining the family. The adolescents may not have developed the skills necessary to assume adult responsibilities and form relationships with other people.

Before any interventions are begun, helping professionals must consider all aspects of the youth's running experience. Runaways require substantial evaluation before any short- or long-term program is planned.

Levels of Intervention for Short-Term Programs

The first priority for the front-line professional—police officer, shelter/crisis center worker, social worker, nurse, or physician—who initially comes in contact with the runaway is to provide safety and meet the youth's physical needs of food, shelter, and health care. The youth needs to know that the basis of this contact is only to provide immediate care and help. From this point, appropriate consultants or agencies (such as departments of youth services or mental health) can be brought in to begin to work with the youth. Because the early involvement of helping agencies is important to any form of effective assistance, front-line personnel need to know which agencies to contact.

Once the immediate physical needs of the runaway are met, helping professionals can begin to assess the runaway's problems. One way of doing so is to use a level-of-intervention approach based on how long the runaway has been away from home.

Level 1 of this approach is aimed at the new runaway who has been away from home less than one month and who has potential for being returned home. Careful assessment concerning the youth's safety in the home needs to be made, particularly if the youth is female and thus at high risk of having been both physically and sexually abused. It is necessary to take time to find out the reason for the youth's running away, the youth's choice of a stable environment, and the viewpoint of the runaway's family. With the preteen runaway, undisclosed sexual abuse must be suspected.

At *level 2,* the multiple runaway who has run away several times and who has been away from home from one month to one year is not only at high risk of having been physically abused in the home, but also of having been abused while on the streets. In addition to the level 1 assessment, these runaways need to be evaluated for general physical and sexual health, drug and alcohol use, and predatory criminal behavior while on their own.

Aimed at the serial runaway who has been away from home for over one year, *level 3* deals with the youth's homelessness as well as with the problems that caused him or her to flee. These youths are generally older and lack satisfactory school and work experience. This group of runaways often contains the "tough kids," the youths who carry weapons and survive on the streets by criminal means. They may be under the influence of another person, such as a pimp or a drug boss, and thus require special protection from these exploiters. In addition to the level 2 assessment, these youths need to be stabilized in a safe environment; helped to use existing skills for work; treated to decrease their tension and anxiety; detoxified for drug and alcohol abuse; and assessed for potential aggression toward themselves as well as toward others.

Because this multilevel approach is based on the youth's runaway experience, one of the first steps is to find out about the nature of the running episode. Helping professionals need to determine why a youth left home for several reasons. The most important of these reasons is to assess whether the youngster is running from an unsafe environment. This assessment may not always be straightforward, as the youth may not even admit to being a runaway. Chronic runaways in particular may not wish to be found. Although record checks are sometimes useful, if parents or caretakers have not reported the youth as missing or runaway, no pertinent information will be available. However, the youth's references to his or her experiences on the street reveal how well and in what manner the youth has been coping. Generally, the longer the runaways have been on the streets, the more adaptive has been their street survival. Helping professionals need to assess how this survival has been attained and at what cost to the runaway.

It is difficult, however, to establish communication with runaways. In general, the longer they have been away from home, the more demoralizing experiences they have had. Such experiences affect their ability to trust, to feel calm, and to feel connected and committed to people and places. Helping professionals need to understand the youths' anxiety and defensiveness. Especially when revealing abusive experiences, youths may have reactions to their own recollections of the trauma. A youth may even attempt to run away from the helping environment, such as the shelter, because of the intensity of his or her feelings about recounting the abuse.

Rapport with runaways is most readily established and maintained when the youths are responded to in a manner that gives them a sense of control, a sense they struggle to attain. Allowing the youth to feel in control of an interview imparts the feeling that he or she can make decisions and choose what will happen. In addition, if a positive relationship does develop between the runaway and a particular staff member, that person should maintain this contact, perhaps as case coordinator, throughout evaluation and treatment stages.

No matter how gently and skillfully directed, questions have great potential for arousing defensiveness in the youth. Because many runaways are inclined to blame themselves unconsciously, they may interpret a question as suggesting that their views are not accurate. This challenges the helper's interviewing skills. However, good rapport with the youth allows the exploration of why a question brought a certain reaction. Stressing that the intention of the question is to clarify what has happened is often useful in dealing with defensive reactions (see table 7–1 for sample questions).

Runaways are often cocky in their responses; this attitude is used as a defense mechanism by the runaway. Rather than confronting the youth, more may be gained by good-naturedly going along with the attitude. Humor is another way of dealing with difficult issues. These young people recoil from direct emotion, and humor may lessen the painful recounting of past experiences.

Physical and sexual abuse are often not easily acknowledged by runaways. They may not answer questions about abuse because they do not realize that they have been victimized, or they may not know that it is neither normal nor legal to be abused. In addition, they may not trust the questioner because they have been exploited in the past or because they may not believe the questioner will really help them. Male adolescents in particular are reluc-

Table 7–1
Sample Questions for Runaways

When running away is suspected

1. Many families fight or argue at times. In your family, what is it like?
2. Kids are afraid to talk about what really has happened to them. I'm wondering if you're feeling like that.
3. Sometimes kids are caught in situations they're afraid to talk about because it might get worse. Have you felt this way?
4. Sometimes parents hit (hurt or beat) their kids. Has that happened to you? What was it like for you?

When running away is disclosed

1. What has gone on at home that contributes to your running away? (Ask for the number of times the youth has run away and for details of events, interactions, and relationships. Ask how discipline is handled in the home, if there is fighting, if anyone drinks, who stays and sleeps in the house and where, what is a usual good day or a bad day for the family, and what TV programs are favorites and why. For example, if the youth says nagging drove him or her out, ask for specifics. Carefully question about physical as well as verbal and sexual force.)
2. Given the events or behaviors that made you run away, how much control do you or other people have over this? (Ask how predictable this type of behavior is, who is responsible for the situation, how changeable these behaviors or events are.)
3. What would have to be different for you to want to stay home? (Ask if things have always been this way in the home and if not, when they changed and what made them change.)
4. What would you need to make this change happen?
5. What would other people need to make this happen?
6. How possible are these changes?
7. What do you want most for yourself?
8. What do you think you need first to get what you want?
9. If you were in my place, what is the most important thing to be said or done for a youth like you?
10. On a scale of 0 to 10 with 10 being the highest, how safe/useful is it for your return home? How safe/useful is it for you on the streets compared with home?

tant to admit to being abused; to them, the abuse reflects on their masculinity. Questions about discipline, fighting, and persons living and sleeping in the home during their childhood may, in an indirect manner, uncover the possibility of abuse (see table 7–1).

It is important to keep several points in mind when interviewing runaways. First, one single interview will not provide all the needed information. It may take many sessions over a long period of time for the runaway to open up. Second, an open mind is essential. Runaways are often judged harshly by others; judgments from the helping professionals will only harm rapport and restrict effective communication.

Once a safe environment is provided for the runaway, front-line responders may refer the runaway for assessment and treatment of deeper problems. Work with the family will be critical for those runaways who are able to return to a safe home. Group work with support of other youths is particularly useful in institutional settings that are known to be safe. Gradually, some youths can resume basic education and job goals.

Long-Term Intervention Programs

It is important to conceptualize treatment programs that fit with the runaway's social setting. We identify three basic settings in which runaways generally will remain for some time: (1) the family, (2) an institution, and (3) a community-based setting. What do we need to provide as minimal models of therapeutic programming for each of these settings?

The Runaway and the Family

The target of intervention in the first setting is the runaway youth and his or her family system. The primary resources for therapeutic efforts and planning are the family itself, the neighborhood, and the school. The sources of program guidance can be the local mental health clinic, a family service agency, a church-sponsored program, or a contemporary self-help program.

The objectives of the therapeutic programming are best derived from careful assessment and evaluation, made in conjunction with the family and the runaway, of the issues that prompted the running away behavior. From our research of reasons for running away, the area of verbal and psychological abuse has been shown to require the skill of a clinician who is familiar with assessing dysfunctional communication patterns within a family context. Patterns of verbal and psychological abuse are subtle. A skilled family clinician is needed to identify the structure of the family dynamics.

This dynamic and structural approach to communication patterns has an immediate outcome objective of changing the experiences among people in the family to more positive and productive ones. Once this is achieved, family members can address the more personal causative factors with sensitivity, compassion, and understanding.

Attention to the family's and the runaway's relationship to important community resources is also important. Issues of school difficulties, independence in work, and other pressing family issues need to be addressed.

When the cause for running away centers around matters of physical and/or sexual abuse with or without the complications of alcohol and substance abuse, it is advisable that a community mental health clinic provide the guidance for the therapeutic program. These situations require multiple modes of simultaneous intervention. First and foremost, external structure of support and resources must be available for the abusers and the victims. Legal services should be included in these resources.

Once family stability is attained and protection and safety are assured, family and individual therapy addressing the precursors to the abuse as well as the impulse to abuse is the next step. For the child who has been abused, aspects of post-traumatic stress syndrome as well as general development issues need to be examined.

One case example illustrates the positive treatment outcome for a runaway living in a family setting. Sally was ten years old when her mother died and fourteen when her father remarried. The woman he married had been friends with the father and his three daughters over a ten-year period. One week after the marriage, Sally was picked up by police for disorderly conduct and for driving a stolen car. Sally and her girlfriend had been planning to run away.

Sally and her family were in family therapy. The focus of the therapy dealt with the meaning of the marriage and the entry of a mother figure into the lives of the tightly knit unit of father and daughters. Sally's complaints centered around the new mother, who tended to set stricter limits than Sally was accustomed to with her father. Much of the therapy focused on the couple's differences concerning limits and adolescent behavior. Because this was the only incidence of disruptive behavior, the therapy had positive results.

The Runaway in an Institution

Institutionalization of a runaway occurs for three major reasons: (1) the youth cannot be returned to a functional family home, (2) the youth's behavior is so disorganized and disturbing that it is dangerous and nonfunctional to the youngster, or (3) the youth's behavior is so deviant that the youngster becomes dangerous to others.

For the runaway who cannot be returned to a functional family and who is placed in a mental facility or in a juvenile detention facility, the immediate therapeutic objective is to assess the youth and move him or her to a safe, community-based residence. Unfortunately, the placement of youths in mental institutions or juvenile detention settings occurs because community-based centers have not been adequately developed.

For the young person in a mental institution, assessment and major symptom reduction are the first objectives. In addition, attention must be paid to a stepwise movement of the youth from the institution to the community. Therapeutic efforts are aimed at utilizing the crisis for a more constructive alignment of psychological defenses and resources. Next, the social context of the institution is used to assess as well as to strengthen positive social interaction. Aspects of education and work are to be supported to whatever reasonable degree possible.

In conjunction with ongoing therapeutic support and educational and work opportunities, a format for evaluating the relative strengths and gains of each youth is needed. This recommendation assumes the availability of a multistage program to move the runaway from a more controlled environment to an independent setting. The severity of the youth's disorganized behavior and the developmental level of the youth become the important parameters for assessing the appropriateness of the various levels of discharge programs.

When complex post-traumatic reactions are present, long-term intervention that first enhances the positive coping abilities of the youth must be instituted. Multiple therapeutic modalities can be used, including group work, individual work, psychodrama, and psychopharmacology.

Within any group of institutionalized runaways, it is possible that youths may be excessively sexually active and may even force others into sexual activities. A similar pattern may occur with regard to physical aggression. This is most frequently the case with youths who have been abused. They may or may not have made the abuse apparent, and their conscious awareness of the abuse experiences may not be available. Nevertheless, their behavior toward others reveals the abuse. Often, this behavior emerges when the youth experiences a protective environment. Thus, it represents a phase in the manifestation of responses to abuse. This behavior is best addressed within the context of the past abuse, with the immediate objective of helping the youth derive self-control so that abusive behavior toward others is stopped.

Youths who are in detention environments usually manifest not only the delinquent behaviors that resulted in their detention, but also some of the behaviors of severely stressed and psychotic youths. There are many factors that curtail therapeutic work with these young people. Often while progress is being made, the youths' juvenile status changes, and they are discharged from confined settings before they have achieved control over their behavior.

The need to explore a variety of treatment approaches for sexually aggressive and other aggressive acting-out behavior is imperative. The attitudes of aggressors, their beliefs about their behavior, and the cues that arouse their aggression must be at the forefront of therapeutic efforts. Easily rationalized violence and abuse have to be challenged. Until the youths can reveal their own vulnerability and generate a sustaining sense of empathy for any victim, they will be unable to control their behavior upon release from the institution. Ongoing family work and educational and skill training are important. After the youth has been discharged from the institution, a program to address the youth's level of self-control, as well as needs for shelter, work, and education, should be instituted.

The tragedy of many youths who are abused and who enter mental health facilities is that the abuse is not evaluated. The following case demonstrates this problem.

Cindy, at age fourteen, attempted to escape her violent, sexually abusive father by taking an overdose of her mother's tranquilizers. She was hospitalized. No one evaluated her reason for taking the drugs, and Cindy was too terrorized to tell why she took them. She was returned home. While Cindy again was being abused by her father, her sixteen-year-old brother discovered what was happening. The two teenagers planned to escape by taking the family car, and they had successfully reached the outskirts of town when Cindy's brother failed to negotiate a turn and crashed into a tree. Both youths were returned to their family and reprimanded by the courts. The abuse remained hidden.

It was not until Cindy seriously considered killing herself at age thirty-two that she realized that her father could no longer control her. She left the house, went to police, filed charges against her father, and brought him to court. She is presently seeking treatment for the long-standing effects of the sexual and physical abuse.

This case also illustrates that within families, abuse is usually multi-faceted. After her disclosure, she learned that her older sister also had been abused by their father and that the abuse was the reason the older sister ran away from home.

The Runaway in the Community

Perhaps the largest population of runaways is to be found residing within the community. Our crowded institutions address only 1 percent of the population that has been abused in some manner. Consequently, our greatest challenge is to establish programs within the community, programs that are aimed at various levels of runaways—runaways who are trying to cope through drugs and prostitution as well as those who are surviving by being predators themselves.

Existing shelters need to be supported by a system of alternative long-term placements. We recommend that these long-term placements utilize self-sufficient, self-supporting living environments whose objective is to provide a haven while the individual pursues those tasks necessary to live an independent life. These tasks may involve seeking therapy for overwhelming symptoms and substance abuse as well as for exploitive and abusive patterns. Voluntary clinics that address sexually violent acting-out behavior need to be available.

In situations involving residential treatment centers and foster homes, settings that are more restricted, support needs to be provided for persons working with the runaways and for the youths themselves. A fair method of monitoring and appraising the services and care provided in these environments needs to be established.

In one example of how a runaway living in the community was able to find help, the nineteen-year-old, white male was arrested for rape and robbery. During the course of trial preparation, a public defender asked the young man if he had ever been raped. Much to the surprise of the youth himself, he admitted that he had been raped and said that no one had ever asked him about it. He went on not only to disclose the abuse, but also to plead guilty and to avail himself of treatment. For the first time, he experienced some hope that he could stop his violent behavior toward others.

Prevention Programs

Long-term prevention programs are aimed at identifying the behaviors and symptoms associated with youths who are ensnared in abusive environments. Media presentations, which often publicize available hot lines, educate young people about the thoughts, feelings, and actions that are indicators of severe reactions to unhealthy family environments. Prevention efforts need to provide young people with assistance in assessing their situations, finding alternatives to any ongoing distress, and modifying symptoms through the institution of healthy coping behaviors.

Additional research is needed for prevention program planning. An assessment tool for case finding of past abuse in runaways was developed from findings in this study. This tool can be used by clinicians and researchers in investigating the problems of runaways. This assessment tool is found in the appendix.

8
Creating a Positive Future for the Runaway

The purpose of our study was to examine the phenomenon of runaway youth in order to gain an increased understanding and to apply this new knowledge to our skills of intervention. In this concluding chapter we review our findings and their implications for successful intervention and ongoing research. We preface this review with two observations on the problem of runaway youth.

Observations on Runaway Youth

Our first observation concerns what we believe to be the flawed public perception of runaways and the meaning generally attributed to runaway behavior. Contemporary American studies as well as this study of Canadian runaways have found that although the adolescent runaway may well be adventurous, rebellious, and stubborn, the youth also is often a victim of a troubled family environment and of multiple abuses. By the act of running away without employment skills or plans, the youth becomes vulnerable to the dangers of survival in the unprotected environment of the street. The runaway is a youth at risk of physical and emotional injury or even death and of sexual and other criminal exploitation. Additionally, he or she is denied the opportunity to live in a safe and stable environment.

Youths who leave home rarely tell their story and are seldom viewed by the general public as vulnerable youngsters. To many people, the runaway's very act of running away from parents or caretakers represents a criticism of the family as an institution; runaways challenge our belief that allegiance to family values guarantees success in adulthood.

Labeling runaways as "failures" or "bad" shifts attention away from the situation from which the youth flees. By dismissing the runaway's behavior as delinquent, we are distracted from what the act of the youth's running reveals about conflicts or family environments. Our society believes in the sanctity of the family, the family's right to privacy, the right of a parent to physically control a child, and the notion that violence is justified and tolerated in certain situations. In other words, society finds that it is the runaway who is out of step. This public attitude contributes to the runaway's feelings of being different and of being alienated, not only from the family, but from friends and peers. In a sense, the runaway is often forced to reconstruct a pseudofamily on the street.

Central to the analysis of running away behavior is the question of whether the runaway problem resides with the youth, the family, or society. One view is that the adolescent is the problem, that the incapable youth drops out or runs away because of personal inadequacies. Another position sees families as responsible for failing to include the child into a normal family life because of various personal conflicts among family members. Another view suggests that youth maltreatment by parents or caretakers is at the root of the problem. Our study showed that child abuse, both physical and sexual, plays a large part in triggering a youth to run away. Still another viewpoint is that society's external protectors of children (e.g., law enforcement, social service, and volunteer agencies) are ineffectual in their roles.

Regardless of which of these factors instigate and perpetuate the runaway problem, it is certain that running away disrupts normal adolescent and family life and is often a sign of problems that need attention. The youth of a society is a valuable resource. Runaways deserve our national attention as an investment in our future stability.

We do not mean to romanticize adolescents who run away from home. Clearly, some do feel hopeless; some have demonstrated disturbing behaviors; some may not be capable of staying in the home or may be a threat to the family. Runaways are often particularly susceptible to being lured into delinquent behavior and are also easy targets for adult predators.

Nevertheless, runaways are often the victims of some sort of abuse, and many of them are frightened. Their voices are rarely heard. Although they have positive potential as upstanding members of society, they do not feel important in their families and are not valued by family members or by social institutions. Life on the street frequently means learning tactics, often criminal in nature, for immediate survival. This further perpetrates the public's image of the runaway as a loser.

Our second general observation concerns the problems facing existing service providers. To provide runaways with a safe haven, communities and agencies have established shelters and halfway houses throughout the country. Some runaways, lonely, terrified, and hungry, come to these places of their own accord, while others are brought there by police. Yet the so-called freedom of life on the streets has a powerful attraction for many runaways. Many youths who do use or who are placed in shelters run away from these havens, despite the risks of living on the streets. In fact, the vast majority of runaway youths choose not to use the crisis centers at all and instead stay briefly with friends before eventually living on the streets.

Runaways as a group present enormous problems for social service agencies that provide them with food and shelter. Some agencies adhere to conventional policies of automatically returning runaways to their homes. If physical or sexual abuse prompted the runaway incident in the first place, the running away will continue. Most community agencies, in their efforts to help runaways with their problems, find themselves overwhelmed with a scarcity of resources. The long-term attention required to treat runaways' problems often sharply conflicts with agency mandates for short-term crisis intervention. The number of runaways who present themselves for complex treatment compromises already seriously limited bed space, forcing some agencies to refuse treatment to youths requesting it.

Local law enforcement is also hampered in dealing with runaway youths. Because a runaway cannot be detained, the police officer who brings a runaway to a shelter may, within a few hours, see the same runaway out on the street again. In addition, police departments with personnel shortages may be forced to place runaways low on their list of priorities, particularly in view of the fact that many youths reported as missing return home of their own accord within a relatively brief period of time.

Mental health professionals, who may detect a running history during an intake evaluation, have seldom been trained to investigate the behavior for its possible linkages to the reason the youth is experiencing psychological problems. This inattention dismisses the seriousness of the symptom and often misses the previously undisclosed victimization.

In short, our system's response to dealing with runaways is often unsuccessful in many respects, partly because it seldom is able to address the cause of runaway behavior, differentiate among the levels and intensity of running behavior, or work cooperatively with other disciplines to coordinate and intervene effectively with the family and the community.

Addressing the Problem of Runaway Youth

Over the years, many of the system responses to runaway adolescents have reflected our society's confusion about the causes and consequences of running away. The ways of dealing with runaways as status offenders have moved from such controlled, confining methods as incarceration without regard for the youth's rights to procedural methods designed to offset this rigidity (e.g., deinstitutionalization).

Today, some people fear that juveniles who run away will be criminalized by their involvement in the criminal justice system and that strong legal steps and protective custody are needed to provide safety for the child. Others argue that the family's sanctity is at issue and that the runaway must be returned home, regardless of the family environment. These groups each can point to inadequacies in the other group's position; the outcome is a stalemate. Our study demonstrates that the cycle of running away is fueled by the social system's ambivalent and incomplete response to the complex issues surrounding the runaway as an individual and the runaway's family crisis.

Social service providers are divided over what they think is the right approach to dealing with runaways. In addition, they are limited in resources. Thus, it is difficult to arrive at a coherent and cooperative strategy to stop the cycle of running away and to create a positive future for the runaway.

Our study underscores that running is, in itself, a traumatic event. Examination of the runaways' accounts reveals the repetitive nature of their running behavior. Given these findings, how can the cycle of running be stopped?

It is clear that immediate efforts at intervention for the youth on the street and the families in crisis deserve the priority attention of existing service and legal agencies. However, the public health dimensions of the problem as a symptom of deeper conflicts and disturbances requires national attention. Public recognition of the problem of runaway youths is essential as a first step in initiating the public policy and procedures needed to deal with the problem and assess its magnitude. Second, it is imperative that relationships among existing resources be reorganized to deal more efficiently with the immediate problems of abused children and runaways on the streets. Third, it is important that there be a commitment of public and private funds for field-initiated research evaluating intervention programs and strategies aimed at the causes and consequences of runaway behavior. These three areas represent a starting effort in creating a more positive future for runaways.

Recognition of the Causes and Consequences of Runaway Youths

Advocacy for Runaways. Runaways are a stigmatized and neglected population. As such, they need advocates to bring their problems to the attention of the public. Governmental recognition of runaways is one step in focusing attention on a population in need. This focused attention does not deny the complexity of the problem or the fact that each human response has an important social context.

National institutes and study groups provide the detailed information that helps determine which factors have negative and positive outcomes for subpopulations of runaways. This data base is necessary for reasonable planning, programming, and developing of social strategies aimed at mitigating the problems associated with runaways. Efficiency and economy of intervention efforts can be more successfully realized when the connections between runaway behavior, parental abuse, and street crime are addressed. In this context, concepts of prevention, early intervention, and rehabilitation give guidance to constructive actions.

Public Recognition Campaign. A campaign for public recognition accomplishes three major tasks: (1) by targeting those people who are unaware of the problems of runaways, it dispels stereotypes regarding the causes and consequences of running; (2) it provides a forum for concerned, knowledgeable citizens who desire guidance in addressing issues facing distressed youths and their families; and (3) it encourages the development of creative public and private financing for strategic programs of service and research.

At minimum, a public recognition campaign should address the following points:

1. Runaway behavior is a public health issue.
2. Runaway behavior is a symptom of family stress, disorganization, and often violent, exploiting patterns of behavior.
3. Family health and the runaway's well-being are not addressed simply by returning the runaway home. Safe and, if possible, self-supporting alternatives to family life need to be established.
4. Front-line respondents to runaways need to make complex decisions regarding the youthful runaway, the family, and the existing social agencies that have responsibility for the runaway.
5. Because of the complex factors contributing to the runaway behavior, the youth's response to aid will vary from cooperation to resentment. A public prepared to modify its immediate expectations will be more successful in engaging these youths in a positive and constructive manner.
6. Legal, social, health, and voluntary services need to be made known to the public. In addition, the public needs to be aware of the scope and limitations of these services.

Reorganization of Relationships

Reorganization of relationships among existing service systems, whether public, private, or voluntary, is needed. In the last fifteen years, mathematical models of research in the social sciences as well as in the health sciences underscore that there is not a simple cause-and-effect relationship between life events and major behavioral reactions. Nevertheless, service efforts are focused on addressing all the causal factors. Agencies tend to work alone and to become insular, protective, and competitive in a nonproductive manner.

It is necessary to find out what does and what does not work for the runaways. This requires an open review of the results of the agencies' efforts and the sharing of this information among the agencies. Such review is necessary at all levels of public, private, and voluntary efforts.

Once the review is completed, the desired outcomes can be described. Differences in efforts can be tabulated, similarities discovered, and gaps identified. From this point, negotiated, cooperative efforts can be developed to reduce the adolescents' need to run from their homes.

The accounts of the runaways who participated in our study indicate that interagency coordination needs to meet five priorities:

1. Most important, runaways need alternative, safe, residential environments.
2. Runaways need immediate relief from the stress they experience. This relief must counter the euphoria they seek via drugs and alcohol.
3. Runaway youths need an economic base to offset their reliance on prostitution and criminal activities for immediate financial support and peer recognition.
4. They need alternative education in order to achieve economic independence.
5. The runaways need multidimensional treatment for their many manifestations of chronic post-traumatic stress disorder.

For those runaways who suffer parental abuse, efforts must be made to address the abuse and provide support services to them and to their families. This support includes shelters for the youths as well as dispositions for the abusing adults. In order to provide this intervention, agencies must be encouraged to participate in efforts of interagency cooperation and evaluation.

Research and Program Evaluation

Large population studies as well as longitudinal studies are needed to explore the many factors that may impede the development of positive family structures. These studies range from the impact of family economics to the effect of violence as portrayed in the mass media. In addition, it is necessary that epidemiological and demographic studies on family violence and runaway behavior be conducted. The long-term biopsychosocial effects of trauma and neglect as they relate to running away also require additional examination.

Collaborative efforts to explore contributing variables as well as the runaway experience itself need to be continued. In particular, researchers must continually consult the youths and the families themselves for their accounts of their experiences. It is from these individuals that we gain our greatest insights into what it takes to survive overwhelmingly negative odds to become a committed, responsible member of society.

Program evaluation has at its foundation the discovery of what works with whom, to what extent, and at what point in the cycle of running. Centralized data analysis centers would help in allowing small agencies a systematic review of their efforts without financially impacting service efforts.

Attitude is another important aspect of program evaluation. Because services are caught in a struggle for existence, they may emphasize positive reports that often minimize the details that might answer critical and ultimately cost-saving questions: With whom is the program most successful? With whom is the program least successful? Might the program be appropriate for a group that is not presently being considered? Consequently, attitudes of openness are needed, attitudes that develop only when agencies feel they can trust evaluation review procedures and interpretation of their reported efforts.

In all areas of research and evaluation, every effort must be made to foster collaboration and cooperation. The delivery system—public, private, and voluntary—needs to work closely with academic research and training centers. In addition, research teams in the areas of law enforcement, government policy, and economics as well as in the traditional areas of the service professions and social research groups must coordinate their efforts.

A Final Word

In summary, a positive future for the runaway youth requires public recognition that runaway behavior represents more than the reaction of wayward or adventurous youths. Today, the children and adolescents who attempt to find sanctuary on the streets are tomorrow's statistics on death, mental illness, or criminal behavior. We as a public must be mindful that runaway behavior patterns reflect complex issues not easily recognized. We must recognize that if the youths of the nation are to act responsibly, the adult population also must act in kind. A first step in this effort is to recognize our abilities and to strive to maintain a spirit of cooperation, tolerance, and positive energy. We can then move to educate ourselves about the needs of the runaways and their families.

Appendix. Runaway Assessment

Interviewer: Please circle appropriate answers and record verbal comments where indicated.

Section A: Personal and Family Information

1. Gender of subject:
   1. Male
   2. Female

2. What race do you consider yourself?
   1. White (not of Hispanic origin)
   2. Black (not of Hispanic origin)
   3. Hispanic
   4. Asian
   5. Other (specify) _____

3. How old were you when you left home for the *first* time?
   _____ years old

4. How old are you now?
   _____ years old

5. How many times have you left home, including the first time?
   _____ times

The next few questions are about your family. First, I'd like to ask you about your family before you left home for the first time, and then I'm going to ask you about your family before you left home the last time.

Interviewer: If subject ran from an institution the last time, make certain information is about last time left home.

6. Just before you left home for the *first* time, would you say that money problems in your family were:
   1. Very bad
   2. Somewhat bad
   3. Occasional
   4. No money problems

7. Would you describe the way your family lived at that time as:
   1. Advantaged
   2. Average but comfortable
   3. Marginal but self-sufficient
   4. Submarginal (some time on welfare)

8. Before you left home for the *first* time, which of the following adult females were living with your family?
   1. Mother
   2. Stepmother
   3. Father's girlfriend
   4. Other adult female (specify) _____
   5. No adult female present
   If no adult female present, skip to question 10.

9. How would you describe your relationship to (female specified above) before you left home that *first* time? *Interviewer: If more than one female is specified in question 8, use the first one named.*
   1. Warm, close
   2. Average
   3. Uncaring, indifferent
   4. Cold, distant
   5. Hostile

10. Before you left home for the *first* time, which of the following adult males were living with the family?
    1. Father
    2. Stepfather
    3. Mother's boyfriend
    4. Other adult male (specify) _____
    5. No adult male present
    If no adult male present, skip to question 12.

11. How would you describe your relationship to (male specified above) before you left home that first time? *Interviewer: If more than one male is specified in question 10, use the first one named.*
    1. Warm, close
    2. Average
    3. Uncaring, indifferent
    4. Cold, distant
    5. Hostile

12. Were these same adults with the family when you left home the *last* time?
    1. Yes
    2. No
    If answer is yes, skip to question 16.

13. How did things change?

14. Do you think that this change had anything to do with you?
    1. Yes
    2. No
    If answer is no, skip to question 16.

15. Why?

Now, I'd like to ask you some of the same questions, but these are about before you left home the last time.

16. How would you describe your relationship to (female specified in question 8) before you left home the *last* time?
    1. Warm, close
    2. Average
    3. Uncaring, indifferent
    4. Cold, distant
    5. Hostile

17. How would you describe your relationship to (male specified in question 10) before you left home the *last* time?
    1. Warm, close
    2. Average
    3. Uncaring, indifferent
    4. Cold, distant
    5. Hostile

18. Just before you left home the *last* time, would you say that money problems in your family were:
    1. very bad
    2. Somewhat bad
    3. Occasional
    4. No money problems

19. How old were you when you left home the *last* time?
    _____ years old

Section B: Runaway Behaviors and Experiences

The next set of questions is about your running away.

1. Did you tell your parent(s) or guardian that you were leaving home the *first* time that you left?
    1. Yes
    2. No

2. What did you tell them, if anything?
3. Did you tell your friend(s) that you were leaving home that *first* time?
    1. Yes
    2. No
4. What did you tell them, if anything?
5. Did you leave by yourself that *first* time?
    1. Yes
    2. No
    If answer is yes, skip to question 7.
6. Whom did you leave with?
    1. Own-age friend
    2. Adult relative (specify) _____
    3. Other relative
    4. Stranger
    5. Other (specify) _____
7. When you left home that *first* time, did you have any specific plans?
    1. Yes
    2. No
    If answer is no, skip to question 9.
8. What were your plans that *first* time?
9. What did you end up doing?
10. Where did you go the *last* time that you left home?
11. What is the farthest that you've traveled?
12. What are the hardest things about trying to live on your own? How did (do) you deal with each of these? *Interviewer: Fill in the lines below.*

Survival Problems	*How Dealt with Problem*
A. _____	A. _____
B. _____	B. _____
C. _____	C. _____
D. _____	D. _____
E. _____	E. _____

13. What are the main dangers of trying to live on your own? How did (do) you deal with each of these?

Danger	*How Dealt with Danger*
A. _____	A. _____
B. _____	B. _____
C. _____	C. _____
D. _____	D. _____
E. _____	E. _____

14. How important were the following reasons to your leaving home for the *first* time?

	Not Important	Somewhat Important	Very Important
A. Being physically beaten	1	2	3
B. Being sexually abused	1	2	3
C. Being thrown out of the house	1	2	3
D. Being taken away against your will	1	2	3
E. Because father (stepfather, or mother's boyfriend) drank too much	1	2	3
F. Because mother (stepmother, or father's girlfriend) drank too much	1	2	3

15. What was the most important reason why you left home for the *first* time? *If answer is "thrown out," ask question 16.*

16. Why were your thrown out of the house?

17. Why did you return home the *first* time?

18. How would you describe your family's reaction to your return that *first* time?

19. How important were the following reasons to your leaving home the *last* time?

	Not Important	Somewhat Important	Very Important
A. Being physically beaten	1	2	3
B. Being sexually abused	1	2	3
C. Being thrown out of the house	1	2	3
D. Being taken from the home against your will	1	2	3
E. Because father (stepfather, or mother's boyfriend) drank too much	1	2	3
F. Because mother (stepmother, or father's girlfriend) drank too much	1	2	3

20. What was the most important reason why you left home the *last* time? *If answer is "thrown out," ask question 21.*

21. Why were you thrown out of the house?

22. Why did you return home other times?

23. Did your family react differently to your return home these times?

24. Do you maintain contact with anyone (write, call, see) from your family now?
    1. Yes (specify) _____
    2. No

25. Would you like to return home now?
    1. Yes
    2. No

26. Why or why not?

27. Do you think that your parents care if you come back home?
    1. Yes
    2. No
    3. Maybe

Section C: Physical Abuse

1. Have you ever been physically beaten?
   1. Yes
   2. No
   If answer is no, skip to next section.

2. How old were you when this happened for the first time?
   _____ years old

3. Who beat you that time? *Ask subject to be as specific as possible (e.g., if answer is "mother," ask if natural or stepmother).*

4. *Enter sex of abuser.*
   1. male
   2. female

5. Approximately how old was this person (abuser) at the time?
   _____ years old

6. Can you tell me exactly what happened that time?
   Probe for triggering incident and nature of physical abuse.

7. How many times did he/she beat you? *If subject's answer is ambiguous, such as "a lot," ask if more than five times. If yes, enter 5 + ."*
   _____ times

8. How many days, months, or years did these beatings continue?
9. Did anyone else ever physically beat you?
   1. Yes
   2. No

   If answer is no, skip to question 16. Enter "1" and ask the next question.
10. Who beat you that time? *Ask subject to be as specific as possible. (e.g., if answer is "mother," ask if natural or stepmother).*
11. *Enter sex of abuser.*
    1. Male
    2. Female
12. Approximately how old was this person (abuser) at the time?
    _____ years old
13. Can you tell me exactly what happened that time?
    Probe for triggering incident and nature of physical abuse.
14. How many times did he/she beat you? *If subject's answer is ambiguous, such as "a lot," ask if more than five times. If yes, enter "5 + ."*
    _____ times
15. How many days, months, or years did these beatings continue?
16. Including the people you mentioned, how many people have physically beaten you altogether?

Section D: Sexual History and Abuse

1. Is it easy or hard for you to talk about sex?
   1. Easy
   2. Hard
2. How did you first learn about sex?
3. How old were you at the time?
   _____ years old
4. Who first taught you about sex?
5. Approximately how old was he/she at the time?
   _____ years old
6. How old were you when you had your first sexual experience?
   _____ years old
7. What was the sex of the person(s) involved in that experience?
   1. Same-sex person(s)
   2. Opposite-sex person(s)
   3. Both opposite- and same-sex person(s)

8. Will you describe that experience for me?
9. Did you enjoy that experience?
    1. Yes
    2. No
10. Why or why not?
11. Have you ever had an enjoyable long-term sexual experience?
    1. Yes
    2. No
    If answer is no, go to question 17.
12. How long did that relationship last?
13. Will you describe that relationship for me?
14. *Enter sex of other person*
    1. Male
    2. Female
15. How old were you when you began that relationship?
    _____ years old
16. How old was the other person?
    _____ years old
17. Have you ever had sex with someone much older than you were at the time?
    1. Yes
    2. No
18. How much older was this person?
19. Have you ever had sex with someone much younger than you were at the time?
    1. Yes
    2. No
20. How much younger was this other person?
21. Have you ever been sexually molested?
    1. Yes
    2. No
22. Have you ever been forced to have intercourse (not prostitution)?
    1. Yes
    2. No
23. Have you ever been forced to pose for pornographic pictures?
    1. Yes
    2. No
    If answers to the above three questions are no, skip to question 39.

Being forced or coerced to take part in sexual activity is sexual abuse. I'd like to ask you several more questions in this area.

24. How old were you when this happened for the first time?
    _____ years old

25. Who sexually abused you that time? *Ask subject to be as specific as possible (e.g., if answer is "mother," ask if natural or stepmother).*

26. *Enter sex of abuser.*
    1. Male
    2. Female

27. Approximately how old was this person (abuser) at the time?
    _____ years old

28. Can you tell me exactly what happened that time?
    Probe for triggering incident and nature of sexual abuse.

29. How many times did he/she abuse you? *If subject's answer is ambiguous, such as "A lot," ask if more than five times. If yes, enter "5 + ."*

30. How many days, months, or years did the abuse continue?

31. Did anyone else ever sexually abuse you?
    1. Yes
    2. No
    If answer is no, skip to question 38. Enter "1" and ask the next question.

32. Who abused you that time? *Ask subject to be as specific as possible (e.g., if answer is "mother," ask if natural or stepmother).*

33. *Enter sex of abuser.*
    1. Male
    2. Female

34. Approximately how old was this person (abuser) at the time?
    _____ years old

35. Can you tell me exactly what happened that time?
    Probe for triggering incident and nature of sexual abuse?

36. How many times did he/she abuse you? *If subject's answer is ambiguous, such as "a lot," ask if more than five times. If yes, enter "5 + ."*
    _____ times

37. How many days, months, or years did this abuse continue?

38. Including the people that you mentioned, how many people sexually abused you?

39. Has anyone ever wanted to take pictures of you in the nude or while having sex, or asked you to be in a sex film?
    1. Yes
    2. No
    If no, skip to question 43.

40. How old were you when this first happened?
    _____ years old

41. Will you describe this experience for me?

42. How many times have you been asked to take part in this type of activity?
    _____ times

43. Have you ever been involved in hustling/prostitution?
    1. Yes
    2. No
    If answer is no, skip to next section.

44. How old were you the first time?
    _____ years old

45. Will you describe that experience for me?

46. Did you enjoy this experience?
    1. Yes
    2. No

47. Why or why not?

48. Did you hustle after that first time?
    1. Yes
    2. No

49. Do you think hustling is dangerous?
    1. Yes
    2. No

50. If yes, will you tell me about some of dangers of hustling?

51. Have you ever gotten hurt while hustling?
    1. Yes
    2. No
    If answer is no, skip to question 53.

52. Will you tell me a bit about that experience?

53. Are you hustling now?
    1. Yes
    2. No
    If yes, skip to question 56.

54. Why did you stop hustling?

55. How long did you hustle altogether?

    Proceed to next section.

56. How often do you hustle?

57. How many tricks do you have in one night?

58. How long have you been hustling altogether?
59. When do you plan to stop hustling?
60. If you did stop, what would you do instead?

Section E: Current and Future Situation

1. If you had to describe yourself in a sentence, what would it be?
2. Tell me five things that you like about yourself.

    A. _____
    B. _____
    C. _____
    D. _____
    E. _____

3. Tell me five things that you don't like about yourself.

    A. _____
    B. _____
    C. _____
    D. _____
    E. _____

4. Name five things that you need right now to get along.

    A. _____
    B. _____
    C. _____
    D. _____
    E. _____

5. Where do you think you'll be in one month?
6. What do you think you'll be doing?
7. Where do you think you'll be in five years?
8. What do you think you'll be doing?
9. If I saw you when you were forty years old, what would you be like?
10. Can you see yourself as a parent with children of your own?
    1. Yes
    2. No
11. If you were a parent, how would you treat your children differently from how you've been treated?

12. If there was one thing in your life that you could have over, what would that be?

13. At the end of your life, when people are talking about you, what are the best things that they could say about you?

14. Is there anything that I haven't asked you about that you think I should have?

15. Now that this is finally over, how was the interview for you? What was good and what was bad about it?

Notes

Chapter 1. Runaway Youth in the Twentieth Century

1. M. Twain, *The Adventures of Tom Sawyer* (1876; reprint, New York: Bantam Books, 1981), 114.

2. *New York Times Magazine,* 10 May 1964, 63–64.

3. Ibid.

4. *Life,* 3 November 1967, 18–29.

5. *Newsweek,* 30 October 1967, 88–89.

6. *Time,* 15 September 1967, 46.

7. *US News & World Report,* 24 April 1972, 40.

8. *Ibid.*

9. Senate Committee of the Judiciary, Subcommittee on Juvenile Delinquency, Hearings on S2829, January 13–14, 1972. 92d Cong., 1st sess., 5–6. Y4.J89/2:R87/2.

10. Ibid, 46–48.

11. *Runaway Youth Act,* July 27, 1972, 92d Congress, 2nd sess. Senate Report 92-1002.

12. *Time,* 27 August 1973, 57.

13. *US News & World Report,* 3 September 1973, 34.

14. House Committee of Education and Labor, Subcommittee of Economic Opportunity, Oversight hearings, 95th Cong., 2d sess., Y4ED8/1:R87.

15. Ibid., 116.

16. *US News & World Report,* 12 May, 1975, 50.

17. "Children's Garden of Perversity," *Time,* 4 April 1977, 109:55–56.

18. "Kiddie Porn," from *60 Minutes* 9 (15 May 1977).

19. *Chicago Tribune,* 15–18 May 1977.

20. Senate Committee of the Judiciary, Subcommittee to Investigate Juvenile Delinquency, Hearings on Protection of Children against Sexual Exploitation, 95th Cong., 1st sess., 27 May 1977, 2.

21. Ibid., 36.

22. Ibid., 31.

23. Ibid., 93.

24. Senate Committee of the Judiciary, *Protection of Children Against Sexual Exploitation Act of 1977, Report on S1585,* 95th Cong., 1st sess., 16 September 1977, 10.

25. U.S. Department of Health and Human Services, *FY 1982 Annual Report to the Congress on the Status and Accomplishments of the Centers Funded under the Runaway and Homeless Youth Act* (Washington, D.C.: Office of Human Development Services Administration for Children, Youth, and Families, Youth Development Bureau), 263. Hearings on Runaway Youth and Missing Children's Act of 1984, House Subcommittee on Human Resources, May 7, 1984, 98th Cong., 2d sess., Y4.Ed8/1:J98/15.

26. House Committee of the Judiciary, *Prohibiting the Sexual Exploitation of Children,* Report to Accompany HR8059, 95th Cong., 1st sess., 1977, H. Rept 95-696, 8.

27. *Time,* 28 November 1977, 23.

28. *Newsweek,* 29 January 1979, 17–18.

29. U.S. Department of Health and Human Services, *F.Y. 1981 Annual Report to the Congress on the State and Accomplishments of the Centers Funded under the Runaway and Homeless Youth Act, Title III of the Juvenile Justice and Delinquency Prevention Act of 1974 (P.L. 93-415), As Amended by the Juvenile Justice Amendments of 1977 (P.L. 95-115) and the Juvenile Justice Amendments of 1980 (P.L. 96-509),* 29. Oversight Hearings on Runaway and Homeless Youth Programs, Subcommitte on Human Resources of the Committee on Education and Labor, 97th Cong., 2d sess., May 5, 1982, pp. 117–144; Y4.Ed8/1:R87/2.

30. Senate Committee of the Judiciary, Subcommittee of Juvenile Justice *Exploitation of Children,* 96th Cong., 2nd sess., 5 November 1981, Y4.J892:J-97-78, 35.

31. Ibid., 36.

32. Ibid., 150–63.

33. Ibid.

34. *Newsweek,* 18 October 1982, 97–98.

35. House Committee of the Judiciary, *Missing Children's Act* of the Subcommittee on Civil and Constitutional Rights, 97th Cong., 1st sess., HR. 3781, Y4.J891:97.33, 82–90.

36. *Missing Children's Act,* 97th Cong., 2nd sess., 12 October, 1982 (P.L. 92-292).

37. Senate Committee of the Judiciary, Subcommittee of Juvenile Justice, *Child Kidnapping,* 98th Cong., 1st sess., 2 February 1983, Y4J89.98–122.

38. Senate Committee of the Judiciary Subcommittee on Juvenile Justice, *Parental Kidnapping,* 98th Cong., 1st sess., 25 May 1983./Y4:J89/2:98–472.

39. House Committee of the Judiciary, Subcommittee on Crime, *Protection of Children Against Sexual Exploitation,* 90th Cong., 1st sess., 16 June 1983, 85–89, 138, Y4:J89/1:98.

40. House Committee of Education and Labor, Subcommittee of Human Resources, *Juvenile Justice, Runaway Youth and Missing Children's Act* amendments 98th Cong., 2nd sess., 7 March 1984, Y4.E8.1:J 98/15.

41. Ibid., 304–13.

42. Ibid., 162–63.

43. Ibid., 162.

44. House Committee of Education and Labor, Subcommittee of Human Resources, *Runaway and Homeless Youth,* 99th Cong., 2nd sess., 25 July 1985, Y4Ed 8/1, 99–23.

45. Ibid., 75.

Chapter 2. Running Away from Home: The Avoidant Path

1. J. Garbarino, J. Wilson and A. Garbarino, "The Adolescent Runaway," in *Troubled Youth, Troubled Families,* ed. J. Garbarino and J. Sebes (New York: Aldine Publishers, 1986).

2. D. Elkind, *Children and Adolescents* (New York: Oxford University Press, 1980).

3. J. Lipsitz, *Growing Up Forgotten* (Lexington, Mass.: Lexington Books, 1977).

4. I. Weiner and D. Elkind, *Child Development: A Core Approach* (New York: John Wiley and Sons, 1972) 187.

5. P. Blos, *On Adolescence* (New York: Free Press, 1962).

6. A. Freud, "Adolescence," *Psychoanalytic Study of the Child* 13 (1958).

7. E. Erickson, *The Challenge of Youth* (New York: Doubleday, 1965).

8. E. Erickson, *Identity: Youth and Crisis* (New York: Norton, 1968).

9. J. Congar, *Adolescence and Youth* (New York: Harper and Row, 1973) 174.

10. A. Peterson and B. Taylor, "The Biological Approach to Adolescence," in *Handbook of Adolescent Psychology,* ed. J. Adelson (New York: John Wiley and Sons, 1980).

11. Congar, *Adolescence and Youth,* 174.

12. C. Chilman, *Adolescent Sexuality in a Changing Society* (John Wiley and Sons, 1983) 16–17.

13. Weiner and Elkind, *Child Development,* 197.

14. Chilman, *Adolescent Sexuality,* 42.

15. J. Piaget and B. Inhelder, *The Growth of Logical Thinking from Childhood to Adolescence: An Essay on the Construction of Formal Logical Structures* (New York: Basic Books, 1958).

16. Elkind, *Children and Adolescents.*

17. Ibid.

18. Erickson, *Challenge of Youth.*

19. Congar, *Adolescence and Youth,* 174.

20. H. Stierlin, *Separating Parents and Adolescents* (New York: Aaronson, 1981) 124.

21. Weiner and Elkind, *Child Development,* 190.

22. J. Youniss and J. Smaller, *Adolescent Relations with Mothers, Fathers and Friends* (Chicago: University of Chicago Press, 1985) 13.

23. J. Katz, "Social Class in North American History," *Journal of Interdisciplinary History* 11 (spring 1981).

24. J. Gillis, *Youth and History: Tradition and Change in European Age Relations* (New York: Academic Press, 1981).

25. See R. Coles, "Charles Dickens and the Law," *Virginia Law Quarterly* (Autumn 1983) 564–587.

26. U. Sinclair, *The Jungle* (New York: Bantam Books, 1981).

27. Youniss and Smaller, *Adolescent Relations,* 77.

28. M. Rutter, *Changing Youth in a Changing Society: Patterns of Adolescent Development and Disorder* (Cambridge: Harvard University Press, 1980) 236.

29. D. Offer and J. Offer, *From Teenager to Young Manhood: A Psychological Study* (New York: Basic Books, 1975).

30. Garbarino, Wilson, and Garbarino, "Adolescent Runaway."

31. D. Elkind, "Exploitation and Generational Conflict," in *Readings in Human Development — Contemporary Perspectives,* ed. D. Elkind and C. Hetzel (New York: Basic Books, 1977) 135.

32. M. Twain, *The Adventures of Huckleberry Finn* (New York: Airmont Books, 1962) 31–33.

33. C. Dickens, *David Copperfield* (New York: Dell Publishers, 1958) 49.

34. Stierlin, *Separating Parents and Adolescents,* 120.

35. Erickson, *Challenge of Youth.*

36. Ibid., 117–18.

Chapter 3. Families of Runaways

1. J. Sprey, "Conflict Theory and the Study of Marriage and the Family," in *Contemporary Theories about the Family,* ed. W. Burr et al. (New York: Free Press, 1979).

2. M. Deutsch, *The Resolution of Conflict* (New Haven: Yale University Press, 1973).

3. M. Straus, R. Gelles, and S. Steinmetz, *Behind Closed Doors: Violence in the American Family* (New York: Anchor Press, 1980).

4. "Twenty-two percent of Survey Were Child Abuse Victims," *Los Angeles Times,* 25 August 1985.

5. P. Fowler, "Family Environment and Early Behavioral Development: A Structural Analysis of Dependencies," *Psychological Reports* 47(1980):611–17.

6. H. Rodman and P. Grams, *Juvenile Delinquency and the Family,* prepared for the President's Commission on Law Enforcement and Administration of Justice, Juvenile Delinquency, and Youth Crime (Washington, D.C.: Government Printing Office, 1967).

7. M. Riege, "Parental Affection and Juvenile Delinquency in Girls," *British Journal of Criminology* 12(1972):55–73.

8. R. Moos and A. Billings, "Children of Alcoholics during the Recovery Process: Alcohol and Matched Control Families," *Addictive Behaviors* 7(1982):155–63.

9. J. Cooper, J. Holman, and V. Braithwaite, "Self-esteem and Family Cohesion: The Child's Perspective and Adjustment," *Journal of Marriage and the Family* 12 (February 1983):153–59.

10. L. Steinbock, "Nest Leaving: Family Systems of Runaway Adolescents," (Ph.D. diss., California School of Professional Psychology, San Francisco, 1978).

11. M. Mirkin, P. Raskin, and F. Antognini, "Parenting, Protecting, Preserving: Mission of the Adolescent Female Runaway," *Family Process* 23(1984):63–74.

12. R. Ressler et al., "Murderers Who Rape and Multilate," *Journal of Interpersonal Violence* 1 (1986).

13. D. Miller et al., *Runaways — Illegal Aliens in Their Own Land: Implications for Service* (New York: Praeger Publishing, 1980).

14. S. Riemer, "A Research Note on Incest," *American Journal of Sociology* 45(1981):566–75.

15. N. Lustig et al., "Incest: A Family Group Survival Pattern," *Archives of General Psychiatry* 140(1966):31–40.

16. E. Elmer, "Child Abuse: The Family's Cry for Help," *Journal of Psychiatric Nursing* 5(1967):332–41.

17. E. Elmer and G. Gregg, "Developmental Characteristics of Abused Children," *Pediatrics* 40(1967):596–602.

18. J. Brown and R. Daniels, "Some Observations on Abusive Parents," *Child Welfare* 47(1968):89–94.

19. J. Weston, "The Pathology in Child Abuse," in *The Battered Child*, ed. R. Helfer (Chicago: University of Chicago Press, 1968).

20. V. DeFrancis, *Protecting the Child Victim of Sex Crimes Committed by Adults* (Denver: American Humane Association, 1969).

21. P. Straus and A. Wolf, "Un sujet d'actualite: les enfants maltraites," *Psychiatrie de l'enfant* 12(1969):577–628.

22. V. Fontana, *The Maltreated Child* (Springfield, Ill.: Charles C. Thomas, 1971).

23. D. Sattin and J. Millet, "The Ecology of Child Abuse within a Military Community," *American Journal of Orthopsychiatry* 41(1971):675–78.

24. M. Toussaint, "La societe et l'enfant victime de mauvais traitement," *Les enfants victimes de mauvais traitements* 28(1971):83–88.

25. D. Henderson, "Incest: A Synthesis of Data," *Canadian Psychiatric Association Journal* 17(1972):299–313.

26. K. Zuckerman, J. Ambuel, and R. Sandman, "Child Neglect and Abuse: A Study of Cases Evaluated at Columbus Children's Hospital in 1968–1969," *Ohio State Medical Journal* 68(1972):629–32.

27. J. Benward and J. Densen-Gerber, "Incest As a Causative Factor in Antisocial Behavior: An Exploratory Study," *Contemporary Drug Problems* 41(1973): 322–40.

28. David Gil, *Violence against Children* (Cambridge, Mass.: Harvard University Press, 1973).

29. Straus, Gelles, and Steinmetz, *Behind Closed Doors*.

30. M. De-Young, *The Sexual Victimization of Children* (Jefferson, N.C.: McFarland, 1982).

31. K. Gruber, and R. Jones, "Identifying the Determinants of Risk of Sexual Victimization of Youth," *Child Abuse and Neglect* 7(1983):17–24.

32. D. Russell, "The Prevalence and Seriousness of Incestuous Abuse: Stepfathers Vs. Biological Fathers," *Child Abuse and Neglect* 8(1984):15–22.

33. D. Finkelhor, *Sexually Victimized Children* (New York: The Free Press, 1984).

34. L. Gordon and P. O'Keefe, "The 'Normality' of Incest," in *Rape and Sexual Assault,* ed. A. Burgess (New York: Garland Publishing, Inc., 1985).

35. K. Keniston, "The Transformation of the Family," in *Crisis in American Institutions,* ed. J. Skolmick and E. Currie (Boston: Little, Brown and Co., Inc. 1985).

36. Tufts New England Medical Center, Division of Child Psychiatry, Family Crisis Program for Sexually Abused Children, *Sexually Exploited Children: Services and Research Project* (1984).

37. P. Stein, *Single Life* (New York: St. Martin's Press, 1981).

38. J. Kohen, C. Brown, and R. Feldberg, "Divorced Mothers: The Costs and Benefits of Female Family Control," in *Single Life,* ed. P. Stein (New York: St. Martin's Press, 1981).

39. H. Lyman, *Single Again* (New York: David McKay Co., Inc., 1971).

40. J. Gordon, "Single Parents: Personal Struggles and Social Issues," in *Single Life,* ed. P. Stein (New York: St. Martin's Press, 1981).

41. A. McCormack, "Risk for Alcohol-Related Accidents in Divorced and Separated Women," *Journal of Studies on Alcohol* 46(1985):240–42.

42. K. Lanning, "Child Molesters: A Behavioral Analysis for Law Enforcement," in *Practical Aspects of Rape Investigation,* ed. R. Hazelwood and A. Burgess (New York: Elsevier, 1987).

43. D. Finkelhor, *Child Sexual Abuse: New Theory and Research* (New York: The Free Press, 1984) 25.

44. E. Farber et al., "Violence in Families of Adolescent Runaways," *Child Abuse and Neglect* 8(1984):295–99.

45. N. Greene and T. Esselstyn, "The Beyond-Control Girl," *Juvenile Justice* 23(1972):13–19.

46. A. Roberts, *Runaways and Non-Runaways in an American Suburb: An Exploratory Study of Adolescent and Parental Coping* (New York: The John Jay Press, 1981).

47. Miller et al., Runaways—Illegal Aliens.

48. Ibid., 3.

49. E. Herzog and C. Sudia, *Boys in Fatherless Families,* DHEW (OCD) 72 (Washington, D.C.: U.S. Government Printing Office, 1971).

50. H. Raschke and V. Raschke, "Family Conflict and Children's Self-concepts, A Comparison of Intact and Single-Parent Families," *Journal of Marriage and the Family* 5(1979):367–74.

51. S. Coopersmith, *The Antecedents of Self-Esteem* (San Francisco: W.H. Freeman, 1967).

52. Raschke and Raschke, *Family Conflict.*

53. D. Watkins, "The antecedents of Self-esteem in Australian University Students," *Australian Psychologist* 11(1976):169–72.

54. Cooper, Holman and Braithwaite, "Self-esteem and Family Cohesion."

55. S. Wolk and J. Brandon, "The Runaway Adolescent's Perception of Parents and Self," *Adolescence* 12(1977):175–87.

56. P. Nilson, "Psychological Profiles of Runaway Children and Adolescents," in *Self-destructive Behavior in Children and Adolescents,* ed. C. Wells and I. Stuart (New York: Van Nostrand Reinhold, 1981).

57. D. Russell, "On Running Away," in *Self-destructive Behavior in Children and Adolescents,* ed. C. Wells and I. Stuart (New York: Van Nostrand Reinhold, 1981).

58. R. Moos and B. Moos, *Family Environment Scale Manual* (Palo Alto, Calif.: Consulting Psychologists Press, 1981).

59. Ibid.

60. R. Moos and B. Moos, "A Typology of Family Social Environments," *Family Process* 15(1975):357–71.

61. W. Penk et al., "Perceived Family Environments among Ethnic Groups of Compulsive Heroin Users," Addictive Behaviors 4(1979):297–309.

62. Ibid.

63. E. Piers, *Manual for the Piers-Harris Children's Self Concept Scale* (Nashville, Tenn.: Counselor Recordings and Tests, 1969).

64. H. Martin, *The Abused Child: A Multidisciplinary Approach to Developmental Issues and Treatment* (Cambridge, Mass.: Ballinger Publishing, 1976.)

65. M. Martin and J. Walters, "Familial Correlates of Selected Types of Child Abuse and Neglect," *Journal of Marriage and the Family* 5(1982):267–76.

66. M. Elbow, "Children of Violent Marriages: The Forgotten Victims," *Social Casework: The Journal of Contemporary Social Work* 71(October 1982):465–71.

67. R. Gelles and C. Cornell *Intimate Violence in Families* (Beverly Hills: Sage Publications, 1985) 55.

68. Millet et al., *Runaways — Illegal Aliens*.

69. L. Steinbock, "Nest Leaving: Family Systems of Runaway Adolescents," *Dissertation Abstracts* 38(1978) 9–B, 4544.

Chapter 4. Social and Psychological Outcomes

1. American Psychiatric Association, *Diagnostic and Statistical Manual of Mental Disorders,* 2nd ed. (Washington, D.C.: American Psychiatric Association, 1968).

2. American Psychiatric Association, *Diagnostic and Statistical Manual of Mental Disorders,* 3rd ed. (Washington, D.C.: American Psychiatric Association, 1980).

3. T. Brennan, D. Huizinga, and D. Elliott, *The Social Psychology of Runaways* (Lexington, Mass.: D.C. Heath, 1978).

4. Ibid.

5. Ibid.

6. K. Meiselman, *Incest: A Psychiatric Study of Causes and Effects with Treatment Recommendations* (San Francisco: Jossey-Bass, 1978).

7. D. Finkelhor, "Sexual Abuse of Boys: The Available Data" (Family Violence Research Program, University of New Hampshire, 1981).

8. J. Herman, "Father-Daughter Incest," *Professional Psychology* 12(1981):76–80.

9. M. De Young, "Counterphobic Behavior in Multiple Molested Children," *Child Welfare* (1984):333–39.

10. K. Gruber, R. Jones, and M. Freeman, "Youths Reactions to Sexual Assault," *Adolescence* 17(1982):541–51.

11. J. Briere, *The Effects of Childhood Sexual Abuse on Later Psychological Functioning: Defining a Post-sexual Abuse Syndrome* (Washington, D.C., 1984).

12. Meiselman, *Incest.*

13. C. Courtois, "The Incest Experience and Its Aftermath," *Victimology: An International Journal* 4(1979):337–47.

14. Herman, "Father-Daughter Incest."

15. Briere, *Effects of Abuse.*

16. S. Eisenstadt, *From Generation to Generation* (Glencoe, Ill.: Free Press, 1956).

17. E. Erickson, "Youth, Fidelity and Diversity," in *Youth: Change and Challenge,* ed. E. Erickson (New York: Basic Books, 1963).

18. A. Burgess, "Rape Trauma Syndrome," *Behavioral Sciences and the Law* 1(1983):97–113. American Psychiatric Association, *DSM III.*

19. Ibid.

20. M. Symonds, "Victims of Violence," *American Journal of Psychoanalysis* 35(1975):19–25.

21. For our assessment of the presence and severity of post-traumatic stress disorder, we compared runaways who said physical abuse was an important reason for their running with those who said that it was not an important reason. The two groups did not differ by age at the time of the interview (approximate mean age of 17 years) or by age when they first or last left home (approximate means of 14 years and 17 years, respectively). They did not differ significantly on the number of household occupants or on the number of brothers or sisters present in the home. Female runaways were more likely than male runaways to cite physical abuse as an important reason for running (58% vs. 34%; $p < .005$), and those who reported physical abuse in the home were significantly more likely to report sexual abuse either before or after leaving home. This was particularly true for females, 80% of whom reported both physical and sexual abuse (as compared with 46% of the male runaways). Because we suspect, but cannot be certain, that the majority of the sexual abuse took place prior to running away, the variable of physical abuse remains the prime indicator of familial abuse in our study. These two groups were compared on the basis of modified versions of scale items that measure subjective distress, life events, and symptomatology. See M. Horowitz, *Stress Response Syndromes* (New York: Jason Aronson, 1976).

22. M. Horowitz, *Stress Response Syndromes* (New York: Jason Aronson, Inc., 1976).

23. J. Garbarino and M. Plantz, "Child Maltreatment and Juvenile Delinquency: What Are the Links" (1984).

24. J. Benward and J. Densen-Gerber, "Incest As a Causative Factor in Antisocial Behavior: An Exploratory Study," *Contemporary Drug Problems* 41(1973): 322–40.

25. J. James and J. Meyerding, "Early Sexual Experiences and Prostitution," *American Journal of Psychiatry* 134(1977):1381–84.

26. T.J. Reidy, "The Aggressive Characteristics of Abuse and Neglected Children," *Journal of Clinical Psychology* 33(1977):1140–45.

27. M. Lynch, "Annotation: The Prognosis of Child Abuse," *Journal of Child Psychology and Psychiatry* 19(1978):175–80.

28. R. Conger, "The Child As Victim: The Emerging Issues of Child Abuse," *Journal of Crime and Justice* 3(1980):35–63.

29. C. Smith, D. Berkman, and W. Fraser, *Reports of the National Juvenile Justice's Assessment Centers* (Washington, D.C.: American Justice Institute, 1980).

30. Herman, "Father-Daughter Incest."

31. M. Silbert and A. Pines, "Sexual Child Abuse As an Antecedent to Prostitution," *Child Abuse and Neglect* 5(1981):407–11.

32. J. McCord, "A Forty Year Perspective on Effects of Child Abuse and Neglect," *Child Abuse and Neglect* 7(1983):265–70.

33. S. Brown, "An Analysis of the Relationship between Child Abuse and Delinquency," *Journal of Crime and Justice* 5(1982):51–55.

34. S. Brown, "Social Class, Child Maltreatment and Delinquent Behavior," *Criminology* 22(1984):259–78.

35. Briere, *Effects of Abuse.*

36. R. Jones, K. Gruber, and C. Timbers, "Incidence and Situational Factors Surrounding Sexual Assault against Delinquent Youths," *Child Abuse and Neglect* 5(1981):431–40.

37. E. Schur, *Crimes without Victims* (Englewood Cliffs, N.J.: Prentice-Hall, 1965).

38. J. Vander-Zanden, *Sociology: The Core* (New York: Alfred A. Knopf, Inc., 1986).

39. G. Adams and G. Munro, "Portrait of the North American Runaway: A Critical Review," *Journal of Youth and Adolescence* 8(1979):359–73.

40. G. Jensen and R. Eve, "Sex Differences in Delinquency: An Examination of Popular Sociological Explanations," *Criminology* 13(1976):427–48.

41. A. Campbell, "What Makes a Girl Turn to Crime?" *New Society* 27(1977): 172–73.

42. R. Jessor and S. Jessor, *Problem Behavior and Psychosocial Development* (New York: Academic Press, 1977).

43. S. Cernkovich and P. Giordana, "A Comparative Analysis of Male and Female Delinquency," *Sociological Quarterly* 20(1977):131–45.

44. D. Steffensmeir, "Sex Differences in Patterns of Adult Crimes, 1965–1977: A Review and Assessment," *Social Forces* 58(1980):1080–108.

45. M. Blumberg, "Depression in Abused and Neglected Children," *American Journal of Psychotherapy* 35(1981):342–55.

46. R. Canter, "Sex Difference In Self-report Delinquency," *Criminology* 20(1982):373–93.

47. D. Silverman, "First Do No Harm: Female Rape Victims and Male Counselors," *American Journal of Orthopsychiatry* 47(1976):91–96.

48. J. Thilmony and T. McDonald, "Rural Sociocultural Change and Its Relationship to the Female Delinquent" (Paper delivered at the annual meeting of the American Society of Criminology, Tucson, Ariz., 1976).

49. P. Giordana and M. Cernovich, "The Economies of Female Criminality: An Analysis of Police Blotters, 1890–1976" (Paper delivered at the annual meeting of

the Society for the Study of Social Problems, San Francisco, 1984).

50. D. Steffensmeir and J. Kramer, "What Happened to the Rise in Female Delinquency? An Analysis of Juvenile Court Data," *Pepperdine Law Review* 6(1979): 1001–16.

51. D. Steffensmeir and R. Steffensmeir, "Trends in Female Delinquency," *Criminology* 18(1980):63–85.

52. Ibid.

53. M. Chesney-Lind, "Judicial Enforcement of the Female Sex Role: The Family Court and the Female Delinquent," *Issues in Criminology* 8(1973):51–59.

54. C. Vedder and D. Somerville, *The Delinquent Girls* (Springfield, Ill.: Charles C. Thomas, 1975).

55. P. Libby and R. Bybee, "The Physical Abuse of Adolescents," *Journal of Social Issues* 35(1979):101–26.

56. J. Orten and S. Soll, "Runaway Children and Their Families," *Journal of Family Issues* 1(1980):249–61.

57. Blumberg, "Depression in Abused Children."

58. A. Robey et al., "The Runaway Girl: A Reaction to Family Stress," *American Journal of Orthopsychiatry* 34(1964):762–67.

59. S. Rogers and A. LeUnes, "A Psychometric and Behavioral Comparison of Delinquents Who Were Abused As Children with Their Non-abused Peers," *Journal of Clinical Psychology* 35(1979):470–72.

60. R. Young et al., "Runaways: A Review of Negative Consequences," *Family Relations* 32(1983):275–81.

61. B. Gomes–Schwartz, J. Horowitz, and M. Sauzier, "Severity of Emotional Distress among Sexually Abused Preschool, School Age, and Adolescent Children," *Hospital and Community Psychiatry* 36(1985):503–8.

62. L. Bender and G. Grugett, "A Follow-up Report on Children Who Had aTypical Sexual Experience," *American Journal of Orthopsychiatry* 22(1952): 825–37.

63. J. Binder and A. Krohn, "Sexual Acting Out as an Abortive Mourning Process in Female Adolescent Inpatients," *Psychiatric Quarterly* 48(1974):193–208.

64. W. Moore, "Promiscuity in Thirteen Year Old Girls," *Psychoanalytic Study of the Child* 29(1974):301–18.

65. W. Arroyo, S. Eth, and R. Pynoos, "Sexual Assault of a Mother by Her Pre-adolescent Son," *American Journal of Psychiatry* 141(1984):1107–8.

66. G. Awad, "Father-Son Incest: A Case Report," *The Journal of Nervous and Mental Disease* 1(1976):135–39.

67. K. Dixon, E. Arnold, and K. Calestro, "Father-Son Incest, an Under-reported Psychiatric Problem," *American Journal of Psychiatry* 135(1978):835–38.

68. F. Kaslow et al., "Homosexual Incest," *Psychiatric Quarterly* 53(1981): 184–93.

69. P. Sarrel and W. Master, "Sexual Molestation of Men by Women," *Archives of Sexual Behavior* 2(1982):117–31.

70. A. Bell and M. Weinberg, *Homosexualities* (New York: Simon and Schuster, 1978).

71. D. Finkelhor, *Sexually Victimized Children* (New York: Free Press, 1979).

72. Finkelhor, "Sexually Victimized Children.

73. G. Fritz, K. Stoll, and N. Wagner. "A Comparison of Males and Females Who Were Sexually Molested As Children," *Journal of Sex and Marital Therapy* 7(1981):54–59.

74. G. Kercher and M. McShane, "The Prevalence of Child Sexual Abuse in an Adult Sample of Texas Residents," *Child Abuse and Neglect* 8(1984):295–501.

75. M. Gross, "Incestuous Rape: A Cause for Hysterical Seizure in Four Adolescent Girls," *American Journal of Orthopsychiatry* 40(1979):704–8.

76. G. Emslie and A. Rosenfield, "Incest Reported by Children and Adolescents Hospitalized for Severe Psychiatric Problems," *American Journal of Psychiatry* 140(1983):708–11.

77. E. Carmen, P. Reiker, and T. Mills, "Victims of Violence and Psychiatric Illness," *American Journal of Psychiatry* 141(1984):378–83.

78. M. Petrovich and D. Templar, "Heterosexual Molestation of Children Who Later Became Rapists," *Psychological Reports* (54(1984):810.

79. C. Wilbur, "Multiple Personality and Child Abuse," *Psychiatric Clinics of North America* 7(1984):3–7.

80. K. James, "Incest: The Teenager's Perspective," *Psychotherapy: Theory, Research and Practice* 14(1977):146–55.

81. B. Fisher and J. Berdie, "Adolescent Abuse and Neglect: Issues of Incidence, Intervention and Service Delivery," *Child Abuse and Neglect* 2(1978):173–92.

82. Steffensmeir, "Sex Differences."

83. Jones, Gruber, and Timbers, "Sexual Assault."

84. I. Lourie, "Family Dynamics and the Abuse of Adolescents: A Case for a Developmental Phase Specific Model of Child Abuse," *Child Abuse and Neglect* 3(1979):967–74.

85. McCord, "Child Abuse and Neglect."

86. D. Paperney and R. Deisher, "The Maltreatment of Adolescents: The Relationship to a Predisposition toward Violent Behavior and Delinquency," *Adolescence* 28(1983):499–506.

87. C. Adams-Tucker, "Proximate Effects of Sexual Abuse in Childhood: A Report on 28 Children," *American Journal of Psychiatry* 139(1982):1252–56.

88. Ibid.

89. M. deYoung, "Self Injurious Behavior in Incest Victims: A Research Note," *Child Welfare* 8(1982):577–83.

90. R. Summit, "The Child Sexual Abuse Accommodation Syndrome," *Child Abuse and Neglect* 7(1983):177–93.

91. M. Sedney and B. Brooks, "Factors Associated with a History of Childhood Sexual Experience in a Non-clinical Female Population," *Journal of the American Academy of Child Psychiatry* 23(1984):215–18.

92. James and Meyerding, "Early Sexual Experiences."

93. Silbert and Pines, "Sexual Child Abuse."

94. B. Schaeffer and R. Deblassie, "Adolescent Prostitution," *Adolescence* 19(1984):689–96.

95. M. Janus, B. Scanlon, and V. Price, "Youth Prostitution," in *Child Pornography and Sex Rings,* ed. A. Burgess (Lexington, Mass.: D.C. Heath, 1984).

96. J. Tillelli, D. Turek, and A. Jaffe, "Sexual Abuse of Children," *New England Journal of Medicine* 32(1980):319–23.

97. C. Rogers and T. Terry, "Clinical Intervention with Boy Victims of Sexual Abuse," in *Victims of Sexual Aggression: Treatment of Children, Women and Men,* ed. I Stuart and J. Greer (New York: Van Nostrand Reinhold, 1984).

98. M. deJong, A. Hervada, and G. Emmet, "Epidemiological Variations in Childhood Sexual Abuse," *Child Abuse and Neglect* 7(1983):152–62.

99. D. Finkelhor, *Child Sexual Abuse: New Theory and Research* (New York: Free Press, 1984).

100. E. Piers, *Manual for the Piers-Harris Children's Self Concept Scale* (Nashville: Counselor Recordings and Tests, 1969).

101. M. Horowitz, C. Schaefer, D. Hiroto, N. Wilner, and B. Levin, "Life Events Questionnaire for Measuring Presumptive Stress," *Psychosomatic Medicine* 39(6) (1977):413–431. M. Horowitz and N. Wilner, "Life Events, Stress and Coping," in *Aging in the 1980's: Psychological Issues,* ed. L. Poon (Washington, D.C.: American Psychological Association, 1980). N. Wilberg, D. Weiss, and M. Horowitz, "Impact of Events Scale: A Cross Validation Study and Some Empirical Evidence Supporting a Conceptual Model of Stress Response Syndromes," *Journal of Consulting and Clinical Psychology* 50(3) (1982):407–414.

102. M. Janus, A. Burgess, and A. McCormack, "Sexual Abuse in the Life Histories of Male Runaways," forthcoming in *Adolescence* 22(86) (Summer 1987).

103. C. Rogers and T. Terry, "Clinical Intervention with Boy Victims of Sexual Abuse," in *Victims of Sexual Aggression: Treatment of Children, Women and Men,* ed. I. Stuart and J. Greer (New York: Van Nostrand Reinhold, 1984), 91–104.

104. A. Burgess and L. Holmstrom, *Rape: Crisis and Recovery* (Bowie, Md.: Prentice-Hall, 1979).

105. A. Burgess and L. Holmstrom, "Sexual Trauma of Children and Adolescents," *Nursing Clinics of North America* 10(1975):551–63.

106. Rogers and Terry, "Boy Victims."

107. R. Pierce and L. Pierce, "The Sexually Abused Child: A Comparison of Male and Female Victims," *Child Abuse and Neglect* 9(1985):191–99.

108. Janus, Burgess, and McCormack, "Sexual Abuse in the Life Histories of Male Runaways."

109. S. Arulanandam, "Runaway Adolescents' Perception of Their Parental Behavior and Environment" (Ph.D. diss., Loyola University of Chicago, 1980).

110. N. Galambos and R. Dixon, "Adolescent Abuse and the Development of Personal Sense of Control," *Child Abuse and Neglect* 8(1984):285–93.

111. J. Gilgun, "The Sexual Abuse of a Young Female in Life Course Perspective" (Ph.D. diss., Syracuse University, 1983).

112. Janus, Burgess, and McCormack, "Male Runaways."

113. Burgess and Holmstrom, "Sexual Trauma."

Chapter 5. Drawings by Runaway Youths

1. A. Burgess et al., "Response Patterns in Children and Adolescents Exploited through Sex Rings and Pornography," *American Journal of Psychiatry* 141 (1984): 656–62.

2. S. Kelley, "The Use of Art Therapy for Sexually Abused Children," *Journal of Psychosocial Nursing* 22 (1984):12–18.

3. R. Pynoos and S. Eth, "Children Traumatized by Witnessing Acts of Personal Violence: Homicide, Rape, or Suicide Behavior," in *Post-Traumatic Stress Disorder in Children,* ed. S. Eth and R. Pynoos (Washington, D.C.: American Psychiatric Press, 1985).

4. A. Wohl and B. Kaufman, *Silent Screams and Hidden Cries: An Interpretation of Artwork by Children from Violent Homes* (New York: Brunner/Mazel, 1985).

5. C. Stember, "Art Therapy: A New Use in the Diagnosis and Treatment of Sexually Abused Children," *Sexual Abuse of Children: Selected Readings* (Washington D.C.: DHHS, 1980).

6. R. Gittelman, "The Role of Psychological Tests for Differential Diagnosis in Child Psychiatry," *Journal of American Academy of Child Psychiatry* 19 (1980): 413–38.

7. J. Falk, "Understanding Children's Art: An Analysis of the Literature," *Journal of Personality Assessment* 45 (1981):465–72.

8. C. Swenson, "Empirical Evaluation of Human Figure Drawings," *Psychological Bulletin* 70 (1978):20–44.

9. H. Roback, "Human Figure Drawings: Their Utility in the Clinical Psychologist's Armamentarium for Personality Assessment," *Psychological Bulletin* 70 (1968):1–19.

10. Burgess et al., "Response Patterns."

11. Gittelman, "Role of Psychological Tests."

Chapter 6. Pathways and Cycles of Runaways: Youths and Their Beliefs about Running Away

1. J. Garbarino, "Troubled Youth, Troubled Families: The Dynamic of Adolescent Maltreatment," in *Research and Theoretical Advances on the Topic of Child Maltreatment,* ed. D. Cicchetti and V. Carlson (Cambridge: Cambridge University Press, in press).

2. J. Rotter, "Generalized Expectancies for Internal versus External Control of Reinforcement," *Psychological Monographs* 609(1966):1–28.

3. A. Cohen and F. Farley, "An Exploratory Study of Individual Differences in Perceptual Centering and Decentering," *Journal of Psychology* 84(1973):133–36.

4. P. McGhee and V. Crandall, "Beliefs in Internal-External Control of Reinforcement and Academic Performance," *Child Development* (1968):91–102.

5. B. Fish and S. Karabenik, "Relationship between Self Esteem and Locus of Control," *Psychological Reports* 29(1971):784.

6. R. Yates, K. Kennelly, and S. Cox, "Perceived Contingency of Parental Reinforcements, Parent-Child Relations and Locus of Control," *Psychological Reports* 29(1975):784.

7. N. Kuiper, "Depression and Causal Attributions for Success and Failure," *Journal of Personality and Social Psychology* 36(1978):236–46.

8. C. Williams and F. Vantress, "Relation between Internal-External Control and Aggression," *Journal of Psychology* 71(1969):59–61.

9. B. Lowery, "Misconceptions and Limitations of Locus of Control and the I-E Scale," *Nursing Research* 30(1981):294–98.

10. Ibid., 296.

11. B. Lowery, B. Jacobsen, and B. Murphy, "An Exploratory Investigation of Causal Thinking of Arthritics," *Nursing Research* 32(1983):157–62.

12. J. Rotter, "Some Problems and Misconceptions Related to the Construct of Internal vs. External Control of Reinforcement," *Journal of Consulting Clinical Psychology* 43(1975):56–67.

13. B. Weiner, "A Theory of Motivation for Some Classroom Experiences," *Journal of Educational Psychology* 71(1979):3–25.

14. D. Russell, "The Causal Dimension Scale: A Measure of How Individuals Perceive Causes," *Journal of Personality and Social Psychology* 42(1982):1137–45.

15. A. Burgess et al., "Response Patterns in Children and Adolescents Exploited through Sex Rings and Pornography," *American Journal of Psychiatry* 141(1984): 656–62.

16. N. Galambos and R. Dixon, "Adolescent Abuse and the Development of Personal Sense of Control," *Child Abuse and Neglect* 8(1984):285–93.

17. Russell, "Causal Dimension Scale," 1140.

18. A. Burgess et al., *Sexual Assault of Children and Adolescents* (Lexington, Mass.: Lexington Books, 1978).

19. J. Herman, "Father-Daughter Incest," *Professional Psychology* 12(1981): 76–80.

20. Burgess, "Response Patterns."

21. Sections of this chapter were adapted from C. Hartman, A. Burgess, and A. McCormack, "Pathways and Cycles of Runaways," *Hospital and Community Psychiatry* 38(2) 1987.

Index

About the Authors

Mark-David Janus, a Paulist priest, is chaplain to the University of Connecticut at Storrs, Ct. Rev. Janus has been working with homeless and runaway youth for the past twelve years. He has served as a pastoral counselor for youth involved in prostitution and pornography; as a consultant on runaway youth for hospital and community agencies; as a researcher and author on several federal research projects concerning homeless youth; and as a member of the boards of directors of Madonna Hall and The Robert F. Kennedy Action Corps, residential agencies for troubled youth.

Arlene McCormack received her Ph.D. in sociology from Boston University in 1983, and her MA/BA in sociology from Boston University in 1981. She has presented and published several works related to the abuse of children. Since 1984, she has been an Assistant Professor of Sociology at the University of Lowell, where she specializes in teaching research methodology.

Ann Wolbert Burgess, R.N., D.N.Sc., is the van Ameringen Professor of Psychiatric Mental Health Nursing at the University of Pennsylvania School of Nursing and Associate Director of Nursing Research at the Department of Health and Hospitals, Boston, MA. She, with Lynda Lytle Holmstrom, co-founded one of the first hospital-based crisis intervention programs for rape victims at Boston City Hospital in 1972. She served as chair of the first Advisory Council to the National Center for the Prevention and Control of Rape of the National Institute of Mental Health, 1976–1980. She was a member of the 1984 U.S. Attorney General's Task Force on Family Violence and on the planning committee for the Surgeon General's Symposium on Violence in October 1985. She was appointed to the first National Center for Nursing Research Advisory Council of the National Institute of Health in 1986. She has coauthored or edited the following Lexington books: *Sexual Assault of Children and Adolescents, Autoerotic Fatalities,* and *Child Pornography and Sex Rings.*

Carol Hartman, R.N., C.S., D.N.Sc. is coordinator of the Graduate Psych/Mental Health Nursing Program at Boston College School of Nursing. For a number of years she investigated the impact of maternal psychosis on children and the role of nursing interventions. For the past seven years she has been working with Dr. Ann Wolbert Burgess on defining the impact of sexual abuse and its influence on psychopathological states and social deviancy.

Judith Wood Howe, M.S., A.T.R., is a graduate of Boston University and Lesley College, Cambridge, Massachusetts. She is Director of the Therapeutic Arts Program in the Department of Psychiatry at The Children's Hospital and The Judge Baker Children's Center in Boston, and a Professional Member of the American Art Therapy Association. Her clinical and research interests include investigation of the potential for art to serve as a diagnostic process with victims of sexual abuse, and exploration of the therapeutic utility of the creative process with eating-disordered adolescents.